Shepherdess
of
Elk River Valley

by

MARGARET DUNCAN BROWN

GOLDEN BELL PRESS
DENVER, COLORADO
1982

Library of Congress Card Number 67-27079

(Printed in the United States of America)

ISBN# 13:978-1125284919

A BAS BLEU EDITION

FIRST EDITION
SECOND EDITION

PUBLISHED BY

GOLDEN BELL PRESS
DENVER, COLORADO

CONTENTS

Preface

During the 47 years that Margaret Duncan Brown lived alone on her Colorado sheep ranch, she kept a diary of her thoughts and exceptional life. She had never submitted anything for publication, except a short piece to The Reader's Digest, that received the First Person Award, September, 1958, entitled "A Little Bunch of Sheep."*

Mrs. Brown died July 30, 1965. As attorney for her estate, my wife being her niece and Executrix of her will, I found her writings stored around the ranch house, mostly on small tablets that she carried in her pockets while tending sheep. I had the enriching experience of organizing the writings into the form here presented.

The writings trace Margaret Duncan, an extremely attractive but pensive young girl, of gentle Southern parentage, to marriage, at age of 18, in 1900, to Thornton Brown, then a mining clerk in Cripple Creek, Colorado. By 1915, her husband had become cashier and resident manager of a bank in Cripple Creek, and the couple were quite active in business and social circles. They decided to become ranchers, and in late 1915, they made a small down payment and moved on 160 acres on Elk River, Routt County, in northwestern Colorado. In 1918 her husband died. She stayed on, and after the hardest of struggles, solely on her own, she paid out the ranch and expanded. When she died, she had a beautiful, improved ranch of 713 acres, debt free. The richest heritage is, of course, her indomitable spirit, her great sensitiveness, perception and philosophy of life, which live in these writings.

Paul E. Daugherty

---

* See Epilogue

Foreword

As the third child of a medical doctor and his wife in a small town in the south, I probably had the typical girlhood.

When quite young, I was said to have "ambition, imagination and an overweening desire for the truth," and that I "struggled with an unnatural timidity, super-sensitiveness and desire for love and approbation." Looking back, I have the feeling that these qualities were not fully understood, my mother having died when I was age eleven. Certain places gave me great pleasure, some incidents great pain to my intense, sensitive nature. I thought older people were principally instruments to thwart me. I even thought God vindictive when I prayed, and I did pray sincerely as a child.

As I grew older, I was admonished about wanting to be alone so much—and for excessive reading, particularly books that were considered advanced for my age. To some extent I felt alone in the family household. My father and my older sister were quite close, and my older brother was bright and very active outside the home. In those years, I fastened my mind and heart on my departed mother.

My diaries started when I was fourteen years of age, and in reviewing them, I note recorded the usual high school parties, with much social life revolving around the church. In early 1897, the name "Dick" begins to appear in the diary with regularity—being Thornton Brown, the only sweetheart I ever had. Typical entries:

> *"January 20. Went to Faust the other night and nearly froze. Have not seen Dick for a century—to speak to, I mean. He went to Goliad and got him a horse. I see him out in the lot with it. He nurses that horse all the time. Poor horse!"*

*   *   *

"February 8. Went to church with Dick last night. Broke my principles, went to the Baptists to see some people baptized—but couldn't see, too crowded. Dick was awfully nice when we came home—only once he got a little spoony. I told him I didn't like M. U. and he said 'Where are your affections, Madge?' I got funny and told him, 'Gone to the races;' I think he was satisfied for the present. And, don't tell anyone but I'm learning to waltz."

By the time I was sixteen years of age I had finished high school and obtained a teaching certificate from a Summer Normal. Dick had taken a job in the mining town of Cripple Creek, Colorado. After I taught school one year, we were married, October 17, 1900.

From 1900 to 1915, we had a full and happy life in Cripple Creek, then a town of ten thousand people. Dick progressed in business, from helper in assay office to mine superintendent. By the time this main story begins, he was cashier of a bank, of nonresident ownership, in which he had complete responsibility.

The Author as a Girl

The Author and Her Husband — Cripple Creek in 1910

*The Author at the
Time of Her Marraige*

Looking for a Ranch — 1914

The Mountain Homestead

Winter at the Ranch

Going It Alone — 1924

The Peace of Late Summer

The Ranch in the Spring

Chapter One

*"The Most Independent Life
in the World"*

> *"My dream is to have a ranch, a life of peace and plenty,
> with considerable leisure, time to read, think and commune
> with nature."*   Diary 1915

By 1915 we had a highly socialized existence, which had begun
to arouse in me a sense of frustration and futility. I longed for a
life more secluded, with time for contemplation and study. On the
other hand, Dick liked our many social activities, but he became
surfeited of the indoor office life and the responsibilities of bank
management. His nerves were beginning to tire.

We talked of acquiring a small ranch. As a youth, Dick had
done a little summer work on a ranch, helping in branding and
round-ups. He was considered a good horse breaker and rider.

In our looking around, we visited a ranch in the Flat-tops of
Colorado. The owners of this lovely foothills cattle ranch, called
"Sunnyslope," had started from below zero, had made the ranch
into a veritable pioneer's paradise of peace and plenty, where the
machine age had not penetrated; a log cabin, no electricity, no
telephone, no gadgets, but everything hand picked from the produce of a lovely vegetable garden. There was venison and grouse
from the hills, trout and grayling from the mountain streams
nearby.

Standing in the carefully tended vegetable garden one sunny
afternoon, I asked the owner innumerable questions about its
care and production; and finally the inevitable question: "What
made you decide on ranching?" His answer was immediate and

1

decisive and convincing: "Because ranching is the most independent life in the world."

I realize now that my mind had been made up for a long time, and the amazing good luck of $1,500, which Dick made on a mining lease, was the impetus that turned every outing or camping vacation into a delightful adventure, with the direct objective of finding a ranch. In those days $1,500 seemed at least. a working sum toward our goal. We were not middle-aged, our forces were in full bloom.

Halcyon days, halcyon trips, any one of which might uncover our heart's desire. Some ranches were too big, some too small, and as to most, our modest amount of cash was insufficient as down payment; but nothing discouraged us. One ranch was found to be infested with loco and completely unfit for livestock. Fortunately, we observed such things in time, due chiefly to Dick's quick perception and business sense.

Finally in the late summer of 1915, harvest time, we went on a camping and fishing trip to northwestern Colorado. The little Elk River Valley of Routt County was literally steeped in beauty. As we had driven down the road a quarter of a mile from an appealing ranch, I, like Lot's wife, looked back. "Oh, Dick," I cried, "That's the place I'd love to have." The cry must have been urgent. Dick stopped the car. "Let's see if we can get it," he said. We parked the car at the side of the road and walked down across the meadow to the two story log house with three picturesque dormer windows. It looked then in structure as it still does to me, like a sturdy little fort, emanating a feeling of security and permanence.

As we walked closer, I remarked: "There isn't another place where the river flows through the yard—that gray old house and the trees—". Dick was seeing the house as I spoke, and he countered: "It is gray and old," he began. "Would you want it otherwise?" I interrupted.

The woman who opened the door was not young and she was crippled, probably with some form of rheumatism. We stated our case. We wanted to buy a ranch. Could this one possibly be for sale? She strangely said, "I dreamed last night that someone would drive down the lane in a big car like yours and want to buy the ranch." Ours was only an ordinary passenger car and it was still

2

parked on the road a quarter of a mile away, but in dreams, as in poetry, one must allow for poetic license. The men were coming in for dinner from the haying and she said she would talk to Henry, her husband, about it. I gathered she was eager to sell and my spirits soared. She invited us to dinner, but we asked if we could park across the river to eat lunch from our camp supplies.

Dick unfurled fishing tackle for one last bout with the trout. I sat beside that singing mountain stream in a state of happy shock over the unprecedented turn of events.

After a while, when our discussion with the ranch owner was resumed, we quickly came to terms. It was all so casual that I wondered if it was make-believe. The total consideration was $8,500, of which $500 was down payment, the balance to be paid at $500 a year. In the trade we obtained a mixed bunch of cattle, some old horse-drawn machinery and a team of horses. I began living in a state of ecstatic expectation. The ranch consisted of 160 acres in a small beautiful valley, with a good meadow and pasture land, well located and with bountiful water, the rushing river only 30 feet from the back door.

There were good range rights; 100 head of cattle could be run by buying a little extra hay. We were 18 miles from Steamboat Springs, a good town, and one mile from a general store. It was one mile to our nearest neighbor, but we could see six other ranch lights at night, which was something I was to appreciate later on.

Back in Cripple Creek, in making arrangements for the move, we started our descent to earth, so to speak. We had to face up to future problems, such as how to raise enough cash to buy a bunch of cattle. Gradually we were beginning to take on a more sober feeling about the realities of our situation.

On October 16, 1915, we started for the ranch, hoping we might be there by dark. But it seemed from the first that the fates were not propitious on that particular day. A cold drizzle greeted us as we drove over the first mountain pass, later turning into pouring rain. At the foot of the pass we met head-on something I had never seen before—a mountain cloudburst directly on the road in front of us and coming toward us, a wall of water a foot or more high. Dick tried to hold the car to the road, but it skidded neatly into the ditch of water at the side of the road and settled securely. The rain continued to pour as we sat water-logged and trapped. It was nearly dusk and we saw no hope of getting the car out of the ditch in the torrential downpour. We had the choice of sitting in the car all night or of taking refuge in a tumbled-down cabin nearby. As we ran for the bridge across the ditch, Dick remarked that the cabin seemed to have more walls than roof.

As we proceeded, we could see that there was actually a roof over about half the cabin and smoke was emerging from the other side. The owner, and our host for the night, was a part-time prospector who kept a donkey in the quasi-room next to him.

The next day, October 17, 1915, was gloomy, with fitful snow. It seemed a portentous day, mine and Dick's 15th anniversary, as we proceeded toward the "place of our dreams."

When we drove in at almost dusk, our feeling of soberness became more intense. The place looked bleak, almost forbidding, in the half-winter twilight. Our predecessor owner was waiting for us and with no preface said, "You'll find ranchin' ain't easy." I answered with some asperity, "We're not looking for ease. We want a permanent home and security and independence, to quit working for other people." Shortly afterwards, he departed.

"I'm glad he wasn't any more articulate," I said, "or we wouldn't have stayed to hang up our hats."

The place was very quiet, only the murmur of the river; and we felt the strangeness of this sudden new independence. Other people had always directed our lives. Now we were on our own. We had broken with the past. We must go on.

I could see that Dick, already questioning the venture, had what traders call "buyer's reaction." "How did we ever happen to do it?" he blurted out suddenly. I replied that it was to get out of a blind alley—that we had been getting nowhere fast, that he was tired of working for others, selling himself for so little. But Dick, sitting in that dingy ranch kitchen, was thinking of the security of the pay check. I knew he thought me visionary as I talked of the brightness and gaiety of just our own life together. Dick loved people.

Then, for a moment, I too, felt the bleakness. The place looked different in October from how it looked in August and

I began to wonder how Dick would stand up to manual labor. The prospect now seemed less than alluring.

I should say here that discovering very soon the complete fallacy of my dream did not wreck all of my illusions. It merely revised some of them. There was no such thing as leisure during that first year on the ranch, as we struggled to get organized. I scarcely had time for my usual amount of reading. As for the communion with nature, there was plenty of that from the very first, but I learned the meaning of that communion the hard way. It was not like the gay, light-hearted camping and outing trips we had taken for years on our vacations. As for the "peace and plenty," I soon discovered those things to be nonexistent for people starting to ranch on a very thin and badly worn shoestring.

The house defied my best efforts. There were no lights, no water until we managed to get a small pitcher pump installed in a corner of the kitchen. The floors were worn and warped; the roof leaked—indeed the roof leaked for many a year before it was fixed! I remember one of the hay men complaining bitterly that he got up to find one of his shoes full of water. There was silence among the rest of the crew until I suggested, "Why don't you put your shoes under the bed?" The man plaintively replied, "It rains in on the bed too."

Milking a bunch of cows to furnish operating expenses, cleaning barns, feeding cattle, shovelling snow off roofs to keep them from caving in, and the eternal ranch routine were almost breaking my husband's spirit. I realized he had no gift for drudgery. When we first talked of coming to the ranch, he had said: "We will have all day to do what we want to do," but we soon found that we did not have time for half the things we had to do. In those first months, it seems to me I only saw Dick under a huge pile of milk buckets. We were too tired at night to think or talk. We went to bed at dark and began the struggle again at daylight. We had never dreamed the winters would be so long and rugged. The snow was several feet deep. Feeding of stock lasted from the middle of November until the middle of April, or longer.

I struggled on with the house, trying to make it habitable. I knew as soon as summer came, company would arrive. Nor was I mistaken. Friends and relatives came in hordes. Our resources were drained, our routine broken up, our privacy invaded to a degree that made me long for the deep winter snows. The care of the vegetable garden and chickens, always a woman's business in a pioneer country, would have been a joy of sorts with time enough to take care of them. But with the cooking for guests and hay crew, the margin grew more and more narrow.

As time went on, our venture began to look shaky. We were barely making the deadline on our payments those first two years. Finances were on the rocks despite all our skimping and the extra money obtained from milk, butter, chickens and eggs. The following excerpt is from my old 1917 diary:

> *"The thing we are trying to do may not seem worth doing, but the urge to do it drives us on. It seems at times sordid and trivial, someone else before us has done it much better. It seems useless to struggle toward the mediocre, but nevertheless we go on and perhaps learn as we go. Perhaps that is what we are here for—for our objective just to learn. The bitterness and cruelties teach us our beatitudes as never we could have learned them otherwise. After a bit of cruelty on our part, or from someone else, we can say 'Blessed are the merciful, for they shall obtain mercy,' with meaning and understanding. There are always times in any undertaking when one only longs to quit, times of profound discouragement, or stress of circumstances that seem too great to cope with. But quitting is usually the hardest way out and must surely leave one with a defeatist attitude. In looking back over the time since we came here, in point of accomplishment, I can see little reason to remain. Actually, we were much more successful in town. It makes me wonder if people instinctively cling to their own self-made crosses, after a problem has been too difficult to solve, yet you still feel that it is individually your own problem, and you struggle on with it."*

We did struggle on, and during the third year, the picture began to look brighter. The cattle had increased. We quit the dairy business, all the milking, and that meant more leisure. There was now little talk of going back to town.

Chapter Two

Stark Tragedy

> *"And when he fell in whirlwind, he went down*
> *As when a lonely cedar, green with boughs,*
> *Goes down with a great shout upon the hills*
> *And leaves a lonesome place against the sky."*
>   *Markham's "Lincoln"*

Shortly after the hopeful turn for the better in our ranching venture I found myself facing the inevitable. To this day I am appalled by the stark tragedy of life in not knowing what the next moment may have in store for us, at the suddenness with which the inevitable strikes at our complete unpreparedness. An innocent looking letter, a casual sentence, may change the whole course of one's life.

Dick had been to Colorado Springs on business, and when he arrived back at Steamboat Springs on Thanksgiving Day, 1918, he had a high fever. He should have gone direct to the Steamboat hospital, but knowing that I was expecting him for Thanksgiving dinner, he made it out to the ranch.

I had heard people talking of the flu epidemic, but we were so busy and I thought so well, that it had little meaning. Dick lasted only five days; and there is no way to describe that final day when the winter was the most severe and the snow the deepest I had ever seen. That day I blotted from my diary.

The next day I took him to Steamboat Springs enroute to Colorado Springs for burial. There had been so many deaths from the flu epidemic that no coffin was available in Steamboat; so the undertaker used some orange crates. As our train proceeded

7

over the Continental Divide we were halted by a breakdown at the snow sheds. Some men were engaged to carry Dick's body to the other side of the Divide to a waiting train. We again travelled east, but the new train was also stalled, this time at Rollinsville. I was able to employ some men at a Rollinsville cafe to take us on to Denver by auto, so we could get a train to Colorado Springs.

After the funeral at Colorado Springs, I started back. I felt as if I was crawling back to the ranch, maimed and hurt, but somewhat numb to sentiments of old Cripple Creek friends who had said, "It's a hard country up there and it takes hard people to live in it".

Reaching Steamboat Springs I checked in at the little country hotel, for banking, legal and dental appointments, before going to the ranch.

When I got back to the ranch the next morning, after a half day's sled ride and a quarter-mile walk, I could hear the cattle in front of the meadow, as I walked down the lane and to the house. It was a low moaning sound, indescribably desolate. Dick's dog sat half way down the lane howling. (He was a one man's dog and it took him a long time to feel any real affection for me). With his howling and the lowing of the cattle in the background, slowed down by the trail with drifted snow, it seemed some time before I reached the house and got the door open with numb hands.

The house was cold. The living room was in mad disorder. I tried not to look at the medicine bottles crowded onto a little stand table, or the couch drawn near the stove where Dick had fought his last battle and lost. The room looked indeed as though a battle had been fought in it. A man's life had been lost. He had been the other half of my life. I began to try to establish order, but I reminded myself of someone striking matches in an ineffectual attempt to light a dark place, a very dark place indeed.

I kept thinking I must ask him what to do about the cattle. They walked back and forth on their feed lot on the meadow in front of the house, making a steady moaning, bellowing sound. Not a wisp of hay was left on the feed lot. I knew the man had been feeding them short. They must wait until the man came from his homestead up in the hills to feed them again in the morning.

"In sickness and in health, until death us do part." Not a

word about loneliness. I did not feel that death had parted us. Merciful tears came and helped the parched, arid wastes of my soul.

I started a coal fire in the old fashioned Franklin Heater, but the chimney was blocked by a heavy snow. It took a long time to melt it, with all doors of the house open to let out the heavy smoke.

Body and soul seemed divorced by the time my body sat lumpishly beside the stove, endeavoring to get warm. My spirit seemed to sit apart, waggishly watching these bodily endeavors. I began opening some mail. "If you need help, let me know." I put the letter down hastily to take up the second. It said, "I know you well enough to know that you won't take help or advice, so I won't offer it." I didn't finish it either. The third letter said, "I don't know a thing about a ranch, but I feel as if I ought to come. If you need me, let me know." I walked over to the stove and dropped the letters in.

The little pitcher pump was frozen. but there was plenty of snow for water. By the time the fire burned and I had gotten a cup of coffee, the homesteader appeared, a little earlier than usual. I was immeasurably cheered by his arrival and also his attitude about getting out a load of hay at once for the cattle. Before he left, I had requested that he leave a load of hay on the sled ready to feed early in the morning, as Dick always did. He said that he would drop by to help me feed during the next few days. I think his sympathy was aroused, and although he knew little about cattle, he was kind. One night, before turning in, I explained to my diary:

> "If you'd lost the person you cared most for in the world, and had to go right on living among things that reminded you of that person, don't you think it would be hard?"

I am only glad that they, who go on, know nothing of the suffering of those who are left—the bewildering feeling of starting a day alone and finishing it alone. It seemed almost impossible to plan alone—there was no initiative except to do something for the live things on the ranch. I just lived each day to shreds, just ragging it out until nothing was left of the day.

9

Looking over my old diary for the period, I note that I was counselling myself to be steady:

"When you are tired, your sense of proportion is apt to be temporarily eclipsed. Wait before making a decision.
Do not set your staff where you cannot find bottom.
There is a time, after such an experience, when there seems no point whatsoever to life. But there must be a point of contact for brave people where we can struggle back into the routine of life, no matter how deep the wounds."

Silence, solitude—it will test a person. During those quiet evenings alone at home, I fought and refought the battle. A decision had to be made. What was I missing? What was I gaining? I reviewed the things of my immediate past—parties, friends, clubs, dances, and best of all, just the sensation of contact with people. I had stood on the street corner in cities and watched the people, at intersections, in big stores. I had enjoyed riding in a car in beautiful residential sections, flowers in brave array—to turn on to a lovely tree-arched avenue. I liked wandering into a library and choosing any book and at night to see a good show. But I remembered, too, the life and the strife behind the rush counter in a big department store. All of this, I measured up against security, solitude, independence of a sort, self-reliance and the livestock. I did not know yet how the scales would tip. I only know that the sudden barking of young coyotes daring me to stay on was an intriguing challenge, as well as finding old bear-sets under deep pines. In my diary is the following entry:

"I once had dreams. I believed in myself and my potentialities. Am I going to give up, supinely submit to trivialities? Haven't I the mental and moral stamina to go on? Of what use are my ancestry, background and tradition, if I am content to remain mediocre? Have I ever done one original thing in my life? Have I added one little bit to the great paean of creation?"

By self-analysis, I knew that there were factors against me—lethargy, longing for ease and serenity. But in my favor were other qualities—ambition, idealism, love of abstract things and longing for self expression.

My diary indicates that thoughts kept coming back to me:

> *"It was bitterly, horribly cold. Perhaps they meant for me to take charge of things at the grave. The cemetery was not bad, it was beautiful, back there at Colorado Springs. In summer I suppose it is ragged and unkempt. In the winter it is covered with snow and it takes a brave, nice stone to show above the snow. I remember I was astonished at the number of nice stones there were. Some people think little of stones, but when it is the one person in the world you cared for the most and it is the last thing you can do for him, it was not a matter of ostentation."*

Vividly I recall a night during that winter when I made the intimate acquaintance with one of the elements. I found out what it meant to be cold, really cold. I was helping open a stack of hay, a frozen stack. This stack resisted the combined efforts of a man, a boy and myself. My efforts at that time were negligible. The boy, to my amazement, discussed the relative discomforts of cold and hunger. The man, a gaunt mountaineer, stolidly worked to break the stack and wished for a pick. A very pale moonlighted scene, pale by reason of the cold, and there was a sleety snow that filled the air like an icy mist, veiling the moon. It was the sort of cold that makes you long ardently for fires. I was past thirty and never before had I really been cold. This seemed an illuminating fact, as I wondered if other people had their feet ache like that, the whole foot ceasing to be a foot, but becoming instead a steady, concerned, unreasoning ache. In my diary I wrote: "Will I ever live through this winter?"

The hard, cold month of December did run its course and my resolutions for 1919 are recorded on the first page of my diary for the New Year:

> *"1. To appreciate everything that holds the smallest bit of joy.*
> *2. To face unpleasantness without flinching.*
> *3. To be fair and just in judging myself, not to expect my friends to make any allowance for me.*
> *4. To try to absorb those qualities that made him so lovable—this above all—to make him live, to commingle them with the qualities in me that he thought strong.*

5. *To try to live today.*
6. *Not to talk too much, not to tell my plans, never to seem too buoyant.*
7. *To be modest and thoughtful—to answer business letters promptly, to acknowledge the smallest kindness.*
8. *Always to talk to other people of their interests, not mine.*
9. *To be forgiving, and make allowances for others when I think they have wronged me. To try to see their point of view. Never to be critical.*
10. *To face difficulties quietly and firmly—never, never to tell my troubles to other people.*
11. *Never to strive for any effect or pose, simply to be myself, my best self, all the time and in every relationship of business and friendship. To be sure that if I do this, each day will be full to the brim, and that there can be no bitterness of dregs. If I cannot be happy, I can at least be useful."*

Chapter Three

Staying On

> *"30 degrees below — 'I embrace this fortune*
> *patiently, since not to be avoided it falls*
> *on me' " — I Henry IV — Diary 1919*

My original ignorance of the real facts of farm and ranch life was appalling. A single tree or a double tree might have been real trees growing in the primeval forest. My mind was fastened on abstractions so completely that I did not see the detail of the foreground. The only thing I knew was how to saddle and ride a horse. It had never occurred to me that a woman who had never made her own bread, milked a cow or raised chickens or planted a vegetable garden would experience any great difficulty in doing those things. Now that I was on my own, my original naivete haunted me.

How should I adjust the mower blades, or sections? One helper called them "blades," the next "sections," the next "knives" —very confusing. I was asked about the "dogs," certainly a strange name for little steel marbles that fit into the wheel hubs, or thereabouts. Or a man would come along and ask, "Where is your pole-ax, double bit?" "Oh, yes!" Casually I hoped there was an axe with a head to it.

I did not know how to measure hay in the stack, or how to irrigate. I asked a cowpuncher, who happened to be at the ranch, which side of a cow to milk. "She will kick if I sit on the wrong side of her to milk, won't she?" "She will, he said with conviction. "You alway milk a cow on the right side." "Of course," I replied, "but do you mean the right side facing the cow or facing with her?" The cow taught me which side by a vicious side swiping, and I also learned that each cow is an individual as much as a person. I think that perhaps the secret of success in handling live stock, the same as people, is to genuinely like them.

"How deep do you plant lettuce seed?" The neighbor stared. She had planted gardens since before she could remember, as had her mother and grandmother before her. She was as utterly at a loss to answer my question as if I had asked her how she ate her dinner, or how she went down into her cellar for potatoes. She literally couldn't tell me.

I began to read government bulletins and poultry books, but I could not always apply my information. No one warned that a setting hen is one of nature's most temperamental creatures and that their maternal instincts are unstable unless severely controlled. Hens deserted their nests, allowed their eggs to get cold, refused to have anything to do with their eggs whatsoever, or even ate their eggs in cannibalistic fashion. My conception of a setting hen had been that you gave her a dozen eggs to sit on, and that in three weeks she gave you a dozen chickens.

And so I struggled on. In those days I ceased to be a lover, and became a menial hand maid. Yet, even then the game still seemed worth the candle. I did not want to go back to town.

Difficulties continued to mount. The harvesting of hay had to be contracted; and labor, during and immediately following World War I, was a serious problem to the rancher. Added to this, any woman, who has the temerity to become an employer, must prove to men that she is capable of getting along with them. There is undoubtedly, at first, a subtle antagonism between man and women in any industrial problem.

Anyone in working at a solution of a problem evolves a philosophy: You can't make a man do your way, but you can make him do his own way to accomplish the same end, and make that way your own way. He may not be actually conscious of it, and since for some reason men seem unable to see a woman's point of view, I decided that I had best try to see theirs. In later years I learned the art of quietly supplementing a helper's ideas with my own. A woman, in working with a man, must always let him keep his self respect, if his work is to be constructively helpful.

"Why don't you put in a hydraulic ram?" At first I attempted to explain that ranching is somewhat like camping. One must enjoy the pleasant features of it enough to endure the unpleasant.

"Why do you stay?" asked one friend who sensed more than any other my attitude. "Because I can sleep," I answered. I had suffered from insomnia before. It was really a pretty good answer, in that I had never been strong physically in my life before coming to the ranch.

By far my hardest task, the one that wore heaviest on my spirits, was the overwhelming job of feeding. There seemed no possibility of finding permanent help. So I began to think of the necessity of selling the cattle. Looking back, I realize that it was not astute business sense that prompted a final decision, but a few episodes that happened almost immediately.

The first was the pink heifer. She was a big, rawboned heifer expecting her first calf. I had heard Dick say that she would make a wonderful milk cow, half Hereford and half Shorthorn. Her calf came sooner than I expected and her bag looked as though it would burst if not relieved by milking. I walked somewhat brashly into her stall in the barn where she had calved. The heifer greeted me with a baleful stare as she quit licking her calf. Before I knew what was happening, she gave an enraged roar, lowered her head and charged to the door. Fortunately the door opened out and I managed to get out of the door just as she hit it from the inside. The terrific impact catupulated me clear across the corral into a snowbank. The heifer then turned back to her calf.

I was bruised and shaken, but no bones broken. After a while I climbed back into her manger from the outside window. She paid little attention to me. The calf was sucking, but one side needed milking. By now her eyes had lost the baleful glare and she continued licking her calf. Suddenly emboldened, I climbed into the stall, relieved the full side of her bag as the calf worked at the other. She was indeed an easy milker. Dick was right—she would make a good milk cow.

The next important incident was the calving of Patsy, one of the older milk cows, also a Hereford-Shorthorn cross, who was usually a benign and amenable creature. She was on a feed lot with the other cattle, which Dick would not have permitted.

At almost dark I noticed her restlessness and knew that she, as we used to say, was "hunting a nest."

I knew that any calf left outside would freeze. I rushed to get her in. She came under heavy protest, but I worried her through the gate and into the barn. I was profoundly puzzled. She walked stiffly as though in pain, but always looking back. After I had her settled, some sixth sense told me to look back in the feed lot—and there, near a providential pile of hay, I found a tiny calf. It was the smallest that I had ever seen. Any experienced hand would have known that it was a twin, but I was not thinking, and mistook it as being premature. I knew the need to get the calf to the house and warm him. I had seen Dick warm them before the kitchen range. I lifted the tiny fellow onto a little hand sled, he being completely iced over and bellowing lustily—a lively premie, I thought. Once in the house, he responded to treatment and I thought surprisingly strong. He took an astonishing number of spoons of milk until I could hunt up a bottle and nipple.

After an interval, I began to remember how strangely Patsy had walked. I ran to the barn with a flashlight and found Patsy with the other calf, already iced over and very quiet. He, too, needed to be warmed up fast. I had put hot water bottles around the fellow in the kitchen, so with a quick refill and a blanket I ran back and began the calf-warming operation in the manger. The once gentle Patsy bellowed furiously and pawed. The water bottles were hung on the tines of a pitchfork and strategically arranged near her front feet, the other near the back spine. I still had to get the blanket over the calf. I had a vision of Patsy mistaking me for a toreador. Remembering Patsy's fondness for alfalfa, I put down from the loft a nice fresh supply. As Patsy ate, I leaned far out over the manger and draped the blanket carefully over the calf, leaving him a good breathing space at the head. After that I rotated between the two calves.

By daylight the barn calf was fairly dry, warm and started on the milky way. Patsy later accepted him with perfect equanimity.

At about this time I think my decision about raising cows was subconsciously in the making. The cow business was a good business, but I was beginning to feel that I was not equal to it. The ranch had no available pasture, only open government range. I shuddered at the thought of calving the bunch, of getting them on

16

the range. Cattle prices were up and I knew that I would have to think this through and quickly. "The slough of despond was sucking me down." Interest on the cattle mortgage was almost due, and I had only nineteen dollars in the bank. I decided to sell the cattle.

The proceeds of the cattle sale were enough to pay off some cattle notes and the forthcoming annual payment on the ranch, and provided a breather on other expenses. The hay would bring in more in the fall. Land values were also beginning to increase. However, I felt that I had nothing to gain by selling the ranch, and my quick sortie and exit from the cattle business had taught me one thing about the future of the place as an asset, namely that it must have more pasture.

My diary began to take on more variety of moods:

> "Just the quiet and peace and comfort of the house—my own quiet place to sit down and think. I suppose living here alone is what other people call queer. No one can know the relief this quiet has been to me. I can stew my own little mess. I have spent the first half of my life explaining. I'm going to start the second half without explanation. But, even at best, it is only the peace that follows a storm."

* * *

> "I long for a pink kimono, a box of chocolates, and the latest, yellowest fiction. I live on horseback in knickers and read stock letters. How I would like riding boots, the kind the leading lady wears in Western Melodramas!"

* * *

> "There's always a south slope."

* * *

> "Pain in chest. Finished 17 ton hay stack, lasted 13 days. Watered horses. Very cold."

Chapter Four

Digging In—Homesteading

"Courage mounteth with occasion"
— King John II — Diary 1920

Since I was already heavy in debt on the ranch, my best chance for additional land was by homesteading. Under the Homestead Law, one could acquire 160 acres of open government land by establishing a homestead site and living on it at least three months each year for three years. There was much competition for the good homestead sites; however, right in front of the ranch a piece of pasture had been overlooked. Being the side of a mountain, it was mostly rocky, brushy land, with choke cherry bushes, service berries, aspen trees and weeds.

This open land had no stock water, such as a creek; but in picking berries on the mountain, I had seen a robin getting himself a drink at a little moist spot, about half way up the side. The homesteader, who helped me, agreed to dig to see if we could get water. He began digging and in a few hours he came to borrow Dick's irrigation boots. The next day we sank a barrel which filled in a short time and the water proved to be the best I had ever known. It was pure, soft spring water. Also, I located another spring further up the mountain, nearer the tip. The discovery of water of course made the homestead much more valuable. I immediately made plans to establish residence, fence it, and do some plowing on a little mesa to prove up and get title.

A man helping with the haying agreed to survey it. I carried the tape line for him, sometimes through scrub oaks and brush so thick that I had to crawl on hands and knees carrying the tape

18

in my mouth. I came to know every square foot of that homestead by the time the little log cabin was built. It was located only a few steps from the first discovered spring, half way up the side of the mountain.

The whole project was something of a challenge, and between the two places, the ranch and the homesead, I had little time to think or brood. I was beginning to feel that I had a break and could now make it. No one else seemed to think so, however. Nobody cheered me on. I even doubted if Dick, my silent partner, would have believed in my ultimate success. When the going became heavy, I used to say to myself, as of Kipling: "If you can trust yourself when all men doubt you—." Also I trusted in the little element of luck that all people who have lived in a mining camp follow, as a "will o' the wisp." They call it their hunch. Dick believed in that, even if he might have doubted my ability as a rancher.

Life on the mountain side that first winter of homesteading was a rewarding experience, a bout with reality. In the snug log cabin I had a good little cook stove, a solid bunk bed, and the then current dog, Spike, a big red stag hound. I also had books, magazines and nuances. I had a view that defies description—the ranch and river, just below, mountains and foot hills to the west, outlined by flaming sunsets at dusk.

No one with appreciation could have helped but yield to the soothing solitude of the deep snows. Wounds of the spirit, somewhat abated, now began to heal. My inclination had been toward self pity, but the complete simplicity of life high up on the mountain, in the little homestead cabin, was like healing balm. The stirrings of a zeal for the whole project began to work like yeast, and life began to have meaning again.

There was even a touch of wildlife on that seemingly desolate mountain side. One night, just at dusk, a flock of lovely brown birds, about like a flock of ptarmigan, flew in and lighted in the snow at the very edge of the cabin porch. I stood very still watching them as they busily scurried about, seeming to walk right on top of the loose snow, pecking as they went. I went back to the cabin to look for crumbs and just as I returned, they dived straight down into the snow and were gone. I walked out trying to find them, but not a trace. It was a disappearing act I have never seen equalled.

A less romantic visitor at night was sometimes the pack rat. On one occasion I could actually feel slithery tails and whiskers near my face. Added to the rat race that went on in the room where I slept, a riotous din went on in the attic-like space above me. It sounded like the rats were moving heavy objects around and rearranging them constantly. Puzzled by this, one morning I climbed up on an embankment back of the cabin and by thrusting my head under the eaves, was able to obtain a good view of the headquarters of operation pack-rat.

The floor was a veritable bone yard. Scattered all about it were the bleached bones of cattle that must have died nearby. What an arduous undertaking it must have been for even a big rat to drag these bones up the embankment and under the eaves. To this day I do not see why the bones should have been dragged around and rearranged every night.

In the middle of the floor was a rat's nest, about a foot in diameter, with irregular, arm-like ramifications extending in several directions. It was a strange structure of dried mud, sticks, grass, string, bits of leather and many small articles, including some of my shiny, new camp spoons, an aluminum thimble from my camp sewing kit and to my further astonishment, a pink wax strawberry from the same sewing kit. Inexplicably, there were also many cakes of old-fashioned compressed yeast in bright wrappers. Indeed it looked as though the rats had robbed a yeast factory! Altogether it was a strange and unaccountable stage setting! Not an actor in sight, but with the coming of darkness, the show would go on!

A stray stag-hound that I called Spike lifted my spirits immeasurably. He had wandered in one day when I was doing chores at the ranch. He made friendly, dignified overtures toward Lad, Dick's dog, who stayed at the ranch and slept in the barn near the horses. When I started back up to the cabin, Spike followed. He was larger than a greyhound, but built like one, except that he had a greater look of brawn and strength, and was taller. He was brindle-red, his coat of short hair, sleek and bright. I had seen his tracks in the snow the day before on the road and wondered about them. I had never seen a dog big enough for such tracks.

From then on Spike was my shadow and he gave me a sense of protection and companionship, invaluable, it seemed to me just then. He slept just inside the cabin door. It was comforting to hear him moving about occasionally in the night. He waited patiently on the snow trail as I worked digging steps on it to make the trip up the hill easier. When I rode horseback, he ranged the whole country side, often disappearing entirely, then dropping suddenly off a steep bank in front of the horse. His grace and strength, when running, was very beautiful and caused much comment.

I should have been prepared for the blow when it fell. A man said he did not know Iverson ever let any of his hounds go. I admitted that Spike had strayed in. The consequence was that Iverson, a rancher and hunter who lived some fifty miles away, appeared to claim Spike. He came just at dusk, and as he drove away down the muddy, half-frozen road, I could see Spike's head over the side of the car, looking longingly back. The cabin was indescribably desolate without him. I tried to get Lad to stay that night at the cabin, but he had his own quarters with the horses. The night seemed very long, the place very still, except for the distant breaking of ice on the frozen river.

Then, just at daylight, scarcely daring to trust the thought, I heard padding on the porch. It was Spike! His paws were muddy and sore from the slush and ice of the half frozen roads, but he ate a prodigious number of pancakes, and flung himself noisily on the floor to sleep off the rigors of his escape and the trip back. Mr. Iverson came again and said tersely that he would have to tie him up. He also said that Red Rover, as he called Spike, was one of the best hounds he had for hunting coyotes and the like. He said it as though I were responsible for Red Rover's defection.

I had thought I might try to buy him, but I knew it was useless. The two days that followed were lonely. I felt as though I had lost my shadow. But the third day, again at daylight, I rushed to the door to let Spike in! A piece of rope hung from his collar, evidently chewed off. One foot was bleeding. This time I phoned Mr. Iverson and tentatively made an offer. He was very short with me and said, "The lazy hound is no good to me. He won't work any more. Just keep him."

There was a demonstration. Security established, I flung my arms around Spike's neck and hugged him. Spike licked my face and whined. The bond between us became even closer. Later on, when I bought sheep, Spike proved invaluable in keeping coyotes away from the flock, and he never showed any inclination to rove around or worry the stock of the neighbors.

With Spike's companionship and aid, I made it through that first winter of homesteading. Things were looking up as spring approached. Only those who live in a part of the country where the seasons are strongly marked can come to know the beauty of approaching spring, or the subtle change from summer to fall. After a few brilliant spring days, the deep snow seems remote, a thing of yester-year. My first stretch on the homestead over, I moved back to the ranch to start the work there. In my diary at this time I find the following:

"Life becomes a series of impressions and the days unfold like the pages of a book—a book too quickly read.
These spring mornings, when the crust is on the snow, when the black birds are singing in the grove of cottonwood trees, the river beginning to break, when there is a certain unmistakable mellowness in the air, seem to be almost inexpressibly beautiful, though wonderful might be better. It is the first stirring of springtime after the long winter. I felt the same urge, to run about on the crust, that evidently possessed the little gray squirrels just out of hibernation."

During the time of this homesteading operation, I also had my usual work at the ranch, including growing fodder for hay making. There had to be irrigation of the meadows, and, in late summer, the hay would face me in no uncertain terms, since a crop of hay meant security for another year. Fortunately there was plenty of water for the irrigation, and I went about it very seriously, feeling as though I must make every blade of grass grow. I was later to learn that failure of hay production on a mountain meadow is almost nil with a reasonable amount of moisture. I have even seen those lovely chains of little mountain meadows high up in the mountains along a small stream, where there wasn't a drop of irrigation and where the deer and elk waded in the tall native grass. In any event, my arduous method produced a good crop and I had the luck to contract the harvesting of the hay to a man who understood his business. By contracting the haying for that season, I did not get the wear and tear of broken machinery, disgruntled field workers, and all the things that arise to harass the man at the top who is trying to get the job done.

Hay sold at $12.75 that first year, a big price then, so that even after I had paid for the contracting, I was secure for another year.

Regardless of my progress with homesteading, and with the hay meadows, the people who had made dire predictions about a woman rancher did not once remove tongues from cheek, so to speak. It is odd, but I was learning that the worst part of being a widow is that people think that once you are on your own, you have involuntarily become incompetent!

One strong and understanding ally was a young woman, a widow who lived with her aged father about three miles away. She operated the ranch, but was heavily hampered by her father's interference. She cheered me on and envied me because I was free-lancing. I envied her because she was experienced and had the physical strength for any sort of performance. Her advice and companionship were invaluable. She drove spirited horses and even broke them. She did things that I did not have the temerity to think of trying. She would drive into the barnyard, where I might be struggling beyond my intelligence and strength, jump out of her buckboard and begin to bring order out of confusion. Inanimate things often seem to have almost human resistence. I saw her pick up the whole back of a wagon once, trying to get it into proper juxtaposition to get the reach back into place. She held it there, telling me to push the reach into the slot, as I called it, but it refused to. I struggled ineffectually and knew she was getting impatient. But the reach would not slide in. Finally I said we would have to get oil. She said no one ever oiled a reach. She looked resigned, but I ran to the shop for oil, and sure enough, the oil did seem to help me get the reach into the slot.

When I would leave the homestead for a visit to the ranch, I often hung the lantern out in the big cottonwood tree in the corral. The sheep seemed reassured to have the light. I recall, also, as I would climb the hill, on looking back, I too would be reassured, for right above the tree, the evening star shone. It could bring a lump into my throat, being a symbol of peace and trust, shining directly above my feeble little beacon in the tree.

During this period of trying to dig in, I am sure that I was looking at myself with even more critical intensity than were any onlookers. I knew that to make it, I would need courage, which is a special kind of fear; that, also, it would take drudgery and prolonged endurance.

My diary entries included:

> *"Patience is a negative virtue*
> *Perseverence is a positive one."*
>
> *   *   *
>
> *"I never think of them as bankers anymore, but only as people who loan money on cattle."*
>
> *   *   *
>
> *"Our remedies oft in ourselves do lie which we ascribe to Heaven!—All's Well—1-1."*
>
> *   *   *
>
> *"Strange new places, mentally. Letters from friends, especially from Cripple Creek, have been like a familiar sign in a strange place."*
>
> *   *   *

Chapter Five

Not All Alone

Not all alone, for thou canst hold
Communion sweet with saint and sage,
And gather gems of price untold
From many a consecrated page.
Youth's dreams, the golden lights of age,
The poet's love, are still thine own.
Then while such themes thy thoughts engage,
Oh! say not thou art all alone.

Not all alone, the lark's rich note
As mounting up to heaven she sings,
The thousand silvery sounds that float
Above, below, on morning's wings.
The soften music evening brings
The cricket's mirth, cicada's glee.
All earth, that harp of myriad strings
Are jubilant with life for thee.

Not all alone, the whispering trees,
The murmuring brook, the starry sky,
Have each peculiar harmonies
To sooth, subdue and sanctify.
The low sweet breath of evening's sigh
Has oft for thee a friendly tone,
To waft thy grateful thoughts on high
And say thou art not all alone.

Not all alone, a watchful eye
That notes the wandering sparrow's fall,
A saving hand is ever nigh,
A Gracious Power attends thy call.
When sadness holds thy heart in thrall
Oft is His tenderest mercy shown.
Seek then the balm vouchsafed to all
And then canst never be alone.

When love goes out of your life, it leaves a vacuum-like void, but everything in life has its compensation. The vacuum is filled to some extent with a vast understanding, unsought perhaps and not actually assimilated. Some people try stimulation of one sort or another, travel or adventure. Reasoning such an experience out to one's self is a safety valve, far more beneficial than much talk. It strengthens resolve and gives a sense of direction for the future, eases and allays our fears, gives meaning and self-reliance toward life. It enables me to recognize some very sturdy and reliable supports.

I love books. When out with the sheep, and during evenings of the long winter months, I had books. All my life I have been an avid reader.

We may not remember a book or whatever we have read, but it contributes to our mental outlook as surely as food supports our upkeep. The mind must be refreshed and stimulated to expand and grow as surely as the body. When I open a new book (and I fairly fondle some of them), I am truly grateful for having it and I wonder what this man has to say and how he is going to say it. That delightful quickening of interest never grows stale in approaching books. In reading, there is no diffidence to overcome, no self-consciousness, no pose as there often is in meeting people.

After a summer of people, no matter how interesting and entertaining, I return to solitude and books with rejoicing. With people, everything that is to be said or needs to be said, can be said in a few days or weeks. Then we are forced to fall back on trivialities; while a good book, usually a man's best effort, tends to hold the reader's interest to its conclusion. If a writer occasionally befools us, at least we do not have to have him in the house again, and no offence is given.

What a treat, a release, to rush home from pasting labels on fruit jars, juggling figures or herding sheep, and then through reading to enter into and associate with the best minds in the world. One can have any sort of company, fit any humor, match wits with the best. One can become interested in the technique of how the thing is done, and the first thing one knows, he will be living in his own mind and lo! freedom! Once a keen sense of perception is developed, the sky is the limit, and no one can take it away. To discover the setting of one quotation, I read the whole book of Ecclesiastes with a zest that I have never applied to any other part of the Bible.

Certain books seem like intimate friends. One can draw on Thoreau for inspiration, Emerson for perception and spiritual values, Maeterlinck's "Wisdom and Destiny" for depth and clarity of expression, Emily Bronte's "Wuthering Heights" for sheer imaginative expression, Kipling for both poetic and prose rhythm, R. Brooke's beautiful poems to remove stings, and, best of all, the magnificent phraseology of the Bible, with its complete plan for life and living.

For trifling sums I have been able to have the greatest of adventures, mental adventures—walking Waldens Pond with Thoreau, following Lowell Thomas to Tibet, singing the songs of Solomon. By good reading one is able to look at the past with new perspective, to the future with hope—to accept the present with faith. Sometimes I feel that my love for books may be overbalancing, as noted in the following diary plea:

"Keep me from caring more for books than for folks."

Nature, wonderful nature, provided another strong support for me. "He restoreth my soul." Here in these foothills is nature at her best—untrammelled, untouched by the hand of man—unexploited as though fresh from the hand of our Creator. Not a picture post card beauty, but a native, natural beauty. No busses rushing through the country, no gift shops and tourist stands, only a few road signs here and there, an old mine shaft or dump, a deserted sawmill without signs of habitation, now overgrown with vegetation—the wonderful sanitation of nature. Little bunches of deer, standing among the pines in the hushed silence, seem to typify and animate a scene with their grace.

Sometimes I have asked myself: Why was I, of all people, chosen for this remarkable experience? Why was I set apart from a humdrum existence in almost unbelievably beautiful surroundings?

There isn't much chance that I will ever be very wealthy, materially; but, in a sense, there is a form of wealth all around us, a harvest that may be garnered—the understanding of nature. Money cannot actually buy it. It comes of experience, and once the soul awakens and true perception and understanding of nature begins to develop, life becomes an adventure. I believe country people have the best chance to get in touch with that rather vague thing we call nature, meaning, of course, the big out-of-doors. But there is usually a bit of it wherever we are, to the right eyes.

This little valley has held most of the answers for me and much bittersweet. On one occasion I was absent for extended hospitalization, in a somewhat distant city. It was slow recovery from surgery. My feeling upon returning is reflected by my diary entry:

"When I unlocked the long-closed door and stepped
Across the threshold, no one visible
Was there to give me greeting, but I felt
The unseen presence (it is always so)
Of those who had been waiting my return.
The silence spoke to me, and in the dusk
I felt the love of family draw close.
Without a word to my receptive sense,
The quiet rooms were glad with welcoming.
I wandered through the still place listening—
And when night came, into its cradle-arms
My old house gathered me and crooned: 'Sleep Well!'
We have been longing for your home-coming."

Truly the old ranch house seems so familiar as to be almost human to me—the river, the contour of the hills intimately dear.

Seeing spring come, I once watched an oriental poppy open, the outer green leaves fall from the bud and the slow unfolding of the inner orange silken leaves. It seemed a miracle. The snow going off the river, then the ice floes breaking up, the rush of the water like a deep song, the accompaniment of the sighing of the wind in the tree, provided a beautiful harmony—the music of the spheres!

Since living here I have seen an island form in the river, first a few pieces of driftwood, logs and the like. Then some silt and dirt and a little grass and brush sprang up from it. Next, a feathery little willow tree and now an island of considerable dimension where the wild ducks nest. All was accomplished without the slightest evidence of effort or design. The result was a beautiful little island.

Sometimes I think many of us humans have little understanding of the great scheme of nature as related to our every day life. A certain stretch of meadow, across the river where I sit to watch the sheep in the fall as they graze, always makes me feel that I do not see very far beneath the surface. I watch the autumn come each year over there, and very graciously the year lives itself out—at first, a gradual tinge of yellow in the bushes and trees along the little creek, the fragrance of dying leaves, a faint change in the summer green of the meadow to a straw color—and then later, to old gold, but it comes so gradually, so graciously that one never knows when the alchemy has taken place. Yet one morning there is a light flurry of snow, not to stay, just to get us accustomed to what is to come. About this time, the little ermine, holding his dinner-dance on the meadow, darting from hole to hole, watching me covertly all the time, is white instead of brown. His vestments of royalty seem to have changed over night. He has taken out his winter's insurance, white like the snow. The coming of autumn is different from the coming of spring, which is definitely perceptible. No matter how closely I watch, I cannot actually see the change. It is like the rabbit that used to come out of the hat.

Some places on the ranch are almost hypnotic to me. I have stood still in the moonlight and looked at a cove in the hills with its sense of mystery that held me in a spell. The cove has a peaceful, yet relentless quality that I have never known elsewhere. It dominates me, commands my entire respect. It gives me a sense of the agelessness of the hills, the endlessness of time, and the complete futility of human endeavor. It makes me believe that the fourth dimension may indeed be a projection of time. Argument, chatter and clatter of conventions, politics, homilies, foibles and fancies all fade here, and there only remains the mystery, the moonlight and the hills, as time itself has stopped. I have stood quietly there listening to the silence and waiting. Usually places where time stands still are places where there is artificiality, of gaiety and of life, but this place makes one remember without the poignancy of regret. It satisfies and fills those places in your mind and being, that must have the substance of dreams, or else life loses its savor. It has an eerie quality in the moonlight; and at twilight, I have seen rabbits play there, giddy as kittens. At dusk I have watched a young doe playing with her fawn, or elk come quietly down the hillside to a salt lick.

I have seen storms of rain and wind lash across that little valley and after the fury of the storm, I have watched the solitary morning star fade before the wonder of the dawn. Then I feel straighter and taller, braced to meet difficulties.

I believe that one must be as fickle as nature to love nature and to understand it, or as elemental and constant as nature to get the real response and satisfaction that is satisfying without danger of satiety. A mountain trail deserves one mood, a rippling stream another; a beaver dam, smooth as a mirror and rife with small furry and winged creatures, a bit of meadow circled in willows and stream, celestial in its peace, is good for another mood.

In my diary, written on a fall day, there is the following entry:

"Weather here in the mountains is like a benediction—a clear, blue sky, bare ground. The work is over for the year, a lull, a period of waiting before the snow comes, then Christmas. The Continental Divide appears so close it seems you can reach out and touch it—the morning star so gloriously beautiful, inescapable with inspiration."

My diary reflects that during the periods of discouragement I often got help:

> "*Today, when somewhat despondent, I happened to catch a glimpse of absolute beauty. A young doe, standing in the meadow grass, seemed to symbolize shyness, grace, complete innocence, and yet reality of nature—sheer living beauty that penetrated the inner consciousness, the furthermost recesses of my mind.*"

The robins in the quakers right outside the door make a great to-do over going to bed, flying through the trees and close to the ground, as though their day's work was not accomplished. I saw a young robin with the thrush spots still on him, pursuing his grasshopper, right to my feet, so intent was he on his meal. A young mother grouse walked along just a few steps from me.

The asters, in bloom, always give me a holiday sense, more than any other flower. The mariposas are rare and lovely as always, but are not human and friendly like the asters.

Another diary entry:

> "*Tired as I was one morning recently, I was awakened by the singing of the birds, and I thought of Carrie Jacobs Bond's 'Mornin' comes, the birds awake, Used to sing so for your sake . . .'—an utterly happy sound.*
>
> *Their night songs sound more plaintive. This basin in the hills was beautiful and peaceful last night. Veiled with twilight, the evening star was like a single exquisite jewel. It seemed perfect to me as I walked home to the cabin after putting the horse in the pasture. The sage brush always gives me the same sensation of intense reality as I walk through it.*"

I rejoice in the exhilaration of spring—when the black birds go where they please—the sound of many robins and of many waters—the river wide open and gamboling over the rocks—sparkling sunshine, not the synthetic sunshine of winter—little furry creatures, chipmunks and squirrels, running about, leaving no trail for their pursuers—the dog, wild with delight to be out of trails of winter—the cats pursuing their predatory way, hoping to catch the small furry ones—a colony of black birds in the willows with their cheerful note of Cheeri-Cheeri!

Besides books, nature and wild life, I have at times had the consolation of prayer. I have tried to remember, as Wendell Phillips once said, "Even one on God's side is a majority."

I think that, finally, I learned to pray. One does not pray naturally. One has to learn. It isn't a matter of belief, but of growth. Some people do not seem to need prayer as others do. They are like nicely adjusted machines, always in balance and timing. With me, it is only by soul-searching talks with my best self that I am able to adjust myself to conditions and to be fair-minded. Only then do I feel in tune with the infinite, and do I know the proud glory in walking alone and trying to do right.

I do not pray any more for things I want, only for strength and for courage to carry on with what I have—not to lose my sense of values or proportion. Even when the little grain of faith seems as small as a mustard seed, I cherish it and pray for its growth.

As expressed in the poem, "Not All Alone," all of the foregoing were looked to as my companions and helpers during the dark, cold winter of 1918, and later. Looking back, I realize that there were other aids.

The great rarely touched strata of the subconscious, that underlies the thought world or mentality, must have helped me. Only when profoundly aroused or touched does one feel the impact of this great realm and power that lies so dormant, and so close. There is in any problem a moment of "entightenment" that makes it seem unsolvable. After we think such problems over from every angle, and fail to break the mental block, we can store the problems for a time in our subconscious, then, like a blinding light, we get enlightenment. The subconscious may work at different times with different people. Just before daylight is my intense hour.

Another factor working with me during the dark days was the urge for self expression through writing. Having kept a diary since I was fourteen years of age, I know that writing is hard work. Any mental work is. With persistent effort, however, as in music or composition, one finds the rhythm—though finding it may be a slow and painful process. I believe there are vibrations of thought as surely as there are electrical vibrations and when one finally and unexpectedly makes the contact, the resulting exultation seems truly magical.

A thought is one of the most tangible things in the world and one of the most real and powerful. To put a thought on paper so others may get it, is an interesting feat. Impressions are even more fleeting than thoughts.

Sometimes I think I write just for the sake of writing—making a record for myself. Perhaps writing fills some strange psychological need in my nature, gives an outlet to some repressed hereditary trait. I believe that the struggle for self expression enables one to overcome even defects of nature, and no drudgery is too enormous in the struggle. Demosthenes, declaiming in his cave to add timbre to his voice, talking with pebbles in his mouth to correct poor enunciation, gives us the picture.

Thoreau has been my consolation, especially when he said: "Nothing goes by luck in composition; it allows of no trick. The best you can write will be the best you are. Every sentence is the result of long probation. The author's character is read from title page to end. Of this he never corrects the proofs."

One cold winter night, I put in my diary:

"I will just keep on fighting and keep on writing."

Chapter Six

The Sheep Venture

"Should I let the steers and cows go at $85, the unweaned calves at $30?"—Diary, 1919

Often I think of my step by step entry into the sheep business. In driving through the adjacent country above the ranch, I had noticed big bunches of sheep. Nothing, it seemed to me, could be more beautiful—the rolling sweeps of sage brush, the sheep broken up, little bunches of ewes and lambs shaded down under the aspens or pines, or drinking at the willow-bordered stream, the herder's wagon with horses grazing nearby. The memory of it kept coming back to me. It was the beginning of the solution of my difficulties.

I heard of twelve head of ewes for sale—big cross-bred ewes, already bred and in fine condition—fat, young and vigorous. They were bred on grass to lamb in March—an advantage. Often the snow is deep here in the mountains in March, but the old cow barn of logs would shelter them all. So I purchased the twelve ewes.

I hung a lantern in the barn as they began to lamb. This was my first intimate association with lambing ewes, but they lambed "like a cat has kittens." One especially big ewe even had triplets. This was a season of ecstacy.

In what she contributed in lifting my morale, Fanny became the star of the little flock. My interest was at the hundred percent pitch and I went to the old cow barn at two hour intervals through the night to watch for lambs, spending much time on my knees rubbing little chilled woolly bundles until they were dry and warm and started on the milky way. The ewes were coopera-

34

tive and seemed to welcome my efforts, often licking my hands as I worked with the lambs.

Early one morning I was working with Fanny's triplets when my friend of the jaundiced eye passed. He came in, and as usual, began critically—"There—she can't feed three," he said. "Maybe not," I answered, "but she can surely count. Everytime I take one away to feed it, she begins to ba-ba terribly, so I leave all three and feed the bottle around to all of them every so often and the hungry one eats."

"I didn't know you knew lambing," he said. "I don't, but the ewes do." Then reluctantly he said, "Pretty cozy," looking around at the barn with the ewes and lambs separated into their panel pens in the clean green hay.

The twelve ewes had seventeen lambs—the only time I ever had one hundred percent survival. Like all beginners, figuring on the basis of twelve ewes, counting lambs and wool, I was sure of the sheep business—or thought I was!

On the strength of this success, I increased my flock to eighty head. Looking back, my temerity amazes me. What astonishes me more, to this day, was the result. These ewes were bred for May lambing, which, of course, was much easier. They would lamb on grass.

There was need of more pasture, to be able to run even a small number of sheep. I had heard of 160 acres of grass, sagebrush pasture that could be bought for $1,200, on time. I paid fifty dollars down, and with an "on or before" contract, got immediate possession. I shall never forget my happy feeling of possession and release as I rode over this small piece of pasture, fully adequate for the sheep and for the lambing. On the 21st of April, we moved the ewes to this place. There was a location cabin of one room and a shed lean-to, a good small horse barn of logs, a good chicken house and cow barn, a good sheep shelter, small but snug, and wonderful spring water.

The buildings would be invaluable. Even I could realize that late spring storms could be disastrous in lambing a bunch of ewes. As lambing time was at hand, I hired a young fellow to stay at the ranch, as I knew I must be with the ewes constantly. The 21st of April was Sunday, Easter Sunday, and added to that, it was San Jacinto Day in Texas, a day of special significance to a native Texan. Never before, nor since, had I seen the grass as advanced as it was that April. It was several inches high in a cove back of the cabin and up on the mountain side.

The boy who helped was to be off on Easter Sunday, and I told him to help me take the ewes as he went down the road toward town. We had only a mile or so of highway to cover, to reach the cabin, and a quarter of a mile more into the pasture place. We started the ewes on the trail, then he drove ahead in his coupe to open gates into the pasture and I followed behind the sheep, with the horse and dogs. The boy had said, "You won't be able to make the sheep go," but once we turned out of the lane onto the highway, the ewes began to trot, then a running walk, then a gallop. They had been moved before in spring and they sensed that grass was the objective of this move. The boy barely had the gates open in time as they poured through and fanned out over the grass. The boy deposited my bedding and camp supplies on the floor of the cabin and departed, saying balefully, "You're going to run yourself to death after them sheep."

Fearing that the boy's warning might be true, I pushed the ewes into the little cove right back of the cabin. In my operation of "making camp," I looked out from time to time, but the ewes had their heads buried in the grass and had scarcely moved. I put in a delightful morning of getting the camp shipshape. I have always liked to make camp and this was an unusually attractive and convenient camp cabin. There were bare floors and log walls, but a good little sheet iron stove that got red-hot with a few sticks of wood, a cot bed, and even a set of rough shelves for food supplies. I had one single shelf for the alarm clock, lamp and a few books, also a home-made table, a bench for the wash-pan and water bucket, and a few kitchen chairs. It was completely adequate. Thoreau, or a pioneer of the very early days, would have thought it luxurious. Added to this, there was a view of what looked out over all creation from the little front porch of the cabin: foothills and mountains piled on mountains, and in the immediate foreground a gentle slope of sagebrush down to the little stream that fed the spring or water supply, willow lined, and inhabited by many birds, one hillside carpeted with anemonies. No habitation could be seen from the door. This was untrammeled nature, all demands of civilization were temporarily lifted, all social amenities for a time discarded or sublimated.

When I looked out at the ewes next time, they seemed alarmingly full. So at about four o'clock, much too early ordinarily, I brought them down to the pole corral in front of the barn. They came "biddably," replete, happy apparently, and lay down. The Easter Sunday stands out in memory as a red-letter day of satisfaction and accomplishment. All of the boy's emotions were worn on his sleeve, and he registered astonishment of a rare sort on his return from town.

The ewes were not due to lamb until May, but with the set-up, good grass and good weather, they went into it without aplomb. The result again was heartening. The ewes lambed easily "on grass." I numbered every ewe as she lambed and numbered the lambs to match. This saved much confusion as lambs care very little which ewe they feed from, but ewes often fight the strange lamb, so it would have been confusing to the caretaker to know where to place the strayed lamb. I took care of them. In point of sheer human endurance, however, the task of lambing this relatively small number was Herculean, done without help. They lambed out in less than two weeks, day or night, rain or shine, at camp or on the adjacent range. By rights it was a twenty-four hour job, but the problem of rest, food and camp chores enter in to those hours.

There were nights when I did not go to bed at all, as the lambing was always heavier at night. To a person less dedicated, those nights would have been very bad. Ewes need help sometimes as human mothers do, and little lambs need care at times, to be sure they were with their mothers and had enough milk. Just when I planned to get a few hours sleep, another ewe would begin to lamb. I had the boy come a few times "to spell me," although he "hated sheep." The only thing to do was to keep going. At last I reached numbers seventy-eight and seventy-nine, and as both were dry ewes, I had a breather. Only the eightieth ewe was left, and I had not lost a lamb. Just before daylight I noticed she was restless, but I was very tired and longed for coffee. I went to the cabin and when I returned a little later, the ewe was making the heartbreaking noise which they do over a little still-born lamb. The survival record was broken.

There is always a sense of profound defeat and discouragement when you stand beside a dead lamb, and watch the pitiful mother try to bring it to life. That one lamb took the bloom off. An old sheep man later said to me, "If you can't look at a dead sheep without feeling, you'll never make a sheep hand."

In any event, my initial experience with sheep helped me to firm up my decision as between cows and sheep. All the while I had been debating whether to get more good milk cows and seriously ship cream. There seemed less risk in cows, and the cream checks were a steady revenue; but I disliked the day to day drudgery of milking. I was now about convinced that I would have a better chance at obtaining some leisure by going all the way with sheep.

After reaching this decison, I knew that I must have enough sheep to make the venture and the expenditure of my best efforts worth while. So I was receptive when I happened to hear of old ewes which a big sheep outfit was selling at $3.75 per head. They were unusually large ewes of the "feather bed" type, literally loaded with wool. Their legs were woolly and their faces and heads were covered with wool, which last proved to be a great nuisance, as they often had to have the wool trimmed from around their eyes to prevent wool blindness. Their woolly legs picked up burrs and mud to a degree, but woolly they were and I knew just how much a spring wool check could help.

The only drawback to getting them was complete lack of capital. The sheep had summered in the hill country above the ranch, and when I heard of them they were to be moved back to Wyoming immediately. I would not have time to get to town to arrange a loan. I did not think that telephoning to the bank was good business. I decided to saddle a horse, go up into the hills to see the sheep, and then work things out from there if the sheep were desirable.

The foreman of the company, from which I was to buy, told me to meet him and the herders at their camp in the hills, twelve miles above my place, at 6:30 in the morning. His tone of voice over the phone indicated his opinion that women were usually late at business appointments, so I arose at 3 a.m.

I had to get off long before daylight on that crisp September morning, so if by chance I managed to buy the sheep, I could bring them back with me. For riding, I chose Buck, a cowhorse that was pastured on the place. It was a snap judgment decision. Buck's owner told me afterwards that Buck resented being taken out of the corral before daylight and always performed as he did with me that morning. He was well-named. He bucked, which was my very first experience with a bucking horse. But everything held together and he bucked out his ill-temper. Finally, while on the run, I got him headed for the big gate onto the road, thinking that if he began to travel, he might stop bucking. He did just that, but he began to travel very fast, at a sharp run and in the opposite direction from which I had to go. He ran for about a half a mile before I managed to turn him and then we made another fast ride toward the foothills where I really wanted to go. Only I did not want to go quite so fast! After a while, however, the road became steep and Buck slowed down and for the rest of the day he was more amenable.

The horse incident gave me a feeling of discouragement. As I rode up the trail I decided I was a tenderfoot, a greenhorn, a novice, a neophite and in no way experienced for the undertaking before me. My spirits were at a sub-zero level, my assurance was virtually non-existent.

But, as dawn was just breaking and we breasted the last steep grade, I jerked Buck to a standstill with no thought of his preferences. He stood still and I realized only then that I should have jerked him sooner! What lay before me was breath-taking, a basin in the hills, surrounded by quaking aspens, service berry, choke cherry and scrub oak brush, all aflame with autumn colors. Frost had been at work up in this higher country. The basin, carpeted with sage brush, was threaded by a creek, fringed with willows. Perhaps a quarter of a mile from where I was, I could see the 2,000 sheep just leaving their bed-ground as the herders, two Mexicans, worked about a roaring fire.

Getting breakfast by such a fire was unusual, I knew, but the air was sharper than ordinary. As I rode closer the aroma of the boiling coffee and broiling mutton was tantalizing and I was really grateful when the herders welcomed me with a heaping plate of food. It included mutton, coffee, white bread, jam and corn meal mush. The herders were talkative and friendly, having heard I was coming, but they had not expected me so early. Neither had I, looking toward Buck grazing gently now in the tufted grass in the sagebrush.

Suddenly all misgivings left me. My mind was made up, as I looked at the sheep. The herders drifted them toward the range corrals, pole corrals right out in the middle of the basin, with cutting chutes so the foreman could separate the sheep in several different bunches merely by swinging dodge gates. The foreman cut out 100 head for me just as they ran, and asked me if I was satisfied. I assured him that I was and that I would send the owner a check. I said it casually, and he replied in kind, to my immense relief. He said that if I could wait until they got the other sheep headed out of the way, he would help me start mine down the trail and across the basin. I told him that I could wait.

I do not remember having any particular trepidation about getting the 100 ewes back to the ranch alone, although they would have to start in exactly the opposite direction from which they were accustomed to going at this time of the year. Sheep are naturally trail-wise and weather-wise; more so, I have since learned, than almost any other animal. Looking back, I am aghast at my own temerity. The foreman and the herders took the whole deal for granted and treated me with the utmost respect.

The foreman helped me expertly across the basin and started the sheep down the steep slope of the road that led toward the ranch, from where I would have about a six mile drive. The foreman was apologetic when he left me, explaining that they were short handed and heading for Wyoming. Before he rode off, he gave me one piece of advice—"Don't try to drive them—just drift them." I assured him I would be all right. He gave me another long, respectful look, and I was alone with the sheep.

In my mood of elation at getting the sheep, I had not the slightest sense of any hazard. I remember that I admired Laddie's expert work, but I know now I did not then fully appreciate the professional quality of it. Also, Buck now obeyed my slightest whim. He stopped when I let the sheep slow down to nip at the bushes and grass along the way. I kept them always moving slowly, not wanting to give them time to think! The lay of the land, as the old-timers say, was favorable too. The road was scarcely more than a trail, a ravine on one side and a steep bank on the other, so that if the sheep were kept "drifting," they showed no desire to leave the road. I now shudder to think of what would have happened if the ewes had scattered down into the ravine or up onto the rough country above the road, or if the sheep dog had not known more than I did.

The only thing I worried a little over was crossing the long river bridge, about a mile from the ranch. To my surprise and relief, however, when I reached it, the sheep trotted peacefully across, without hesitation. When I mentioned this to an old cow man, he said, "Them sheep! Why, they're used to them cable bridges up in the high country. They didn't know they was crossin' a bridge." So about the middle of the afternoon Laddie expertly herded the ewes through the big gate which was providentially wide open due to my argument with Buck before daylight.

I put the sheep into a small pasture near the house and that night I went to sleep, tired and relaxed, thinking I must get to town next day to see what I could do about making payment for them. I knew the ewes were old or they would not have sold at that price, but I thought they were serviceable, which proved to be correct. There is, however, always a hazard in any business deal, I suppose. At that stage, my experience with any kind of business was limited.

Very early next morning I went out to look at the ewes. My astonishment turned to consternation when I leaned on the pasture fence. Eleven of the ewes lay broadside, scattered through the bunch. I went weak as I looked and realized instantly that those ewes were dead. I have never seen ewes look deader. Then I gathered myself together and ran to look. Something I had heard came back to me—that sheep sometimes got a sort of yellow jaundice disease from eating too much scrub oak in the fall just as frost hits the brush. I had no doubt that this was it. I got the rest of the new bunch segregated at once, where they would not be near the ranch sheep. A neighbor came by and looked at the dead ewes, and so fast is news transmitted by the grapevine that the owner of the sheep was at the ranch in a little while. He had been at the general store a mile above the ranch when the neighbor went in and told the story.

The owner confirmed my suspicions of its being the "yellow disease," as it was commonly called. He doubted it would get any more sheep since now they were no longer pastured on the scrub oak. He said that he was willing to take half the loss. I told him that I had heard the usual sheep loss, business loss, was ten percent. I added that I did not want to be a "short sport." Someone came along and called him off just then, so there was no further discussion, nor was anything said about payment for the sheep. (He would likely give me time. The wool would take care of that!) The thought of the wool steadied me.

The next morning I went to town to raise money to pay for the sheep, and also for taxes on the ranch, which would soon be advertised if not paid. The man I usually dealt with at the bank was gone. Dispirited, I felt my morale slip lower and lower as, poker-faced, I stated my case to the cashier. I explained that I needed enough money to pay for the sheep, for taxes and for operating expenses. Without comment, he wrote for a moment and pushed over a note for me to sign, saying he would forward the mortgage in a day or so for me to sign. It was as easy as that; but the reaction from worry left me limp.

The neighbor I rode home with said she didn't see how anyone could stand working alone. I assured her that I was too busy to think about it; but later it came back to me, and I tried to rationalize the fact that I was actually no longer lonely. Anyone alone naturally becomes somewhat analytical, even about himself. I believe I had come to think of myself as working for someone else, or almost that.

The concepts of business, at first a closed book to me, began to take on meaning. Something Dick had once said came back to me: "Don't try to get your way all at once. Get your wedge in and work from there." I remembered this many times, but when it seemed impossible to deal with people, I found compromise to be invaluable in working things through. Perhaps compromise is the wedge! Another thing I learned, that helped in many relatively small deals, was that one must cultivate a relaxed attitude. No one likes to deal with a do-or-die, rule-or-ruin sort of person.

Although advice from others helped, I found that I must make my own decisions and then trust my own judgment. Each one knows his own limitations or capabilities, his own physical and mental resources, as no one else can know them. He must be honest enough to take stock of them. Good judgment is said to be compounded of careful consideration of all the facts at hand, plus past experience. Naturally it frightened me to think of my complete lack of experience!

Friends may often wonder why I have pursued a certain course of action. Sometimes I wonder myself. I believe, however, that deep in my consciousness, there has been a sense of expediency. There have been small events, half-admitted decisions, and finally the urgent demand of some emergency that gives one the impetus to act and to act decisively. This action often comes, as I say, from a culmination of events. Someone has said that there are three reasons why we do things—the reason we tell our friends, the reason we tell ourselves, and the real reason. But I think that the matter of expediency has the greatest bearing on our actions. With only certain courses of action open to us, there is, of course, the important factor—the ability to choose, or judgment. This ability to choose, although perhaps one of the lesser gifts of character, is an outgrowth of discernment and can yield great returns.

My old diaries for that period contain no clear reasoned explanations on my decision. Instead, there are mostly just long lists of chores to do, and observations like:

> *"Some days are good, some days are bad. I never have much choice of what I will do next. Of the ten most pressing things, I choose the most important thing and then go about it—hampered by the consciousness of the nine things left undone. Like the rabbit in 'Alice,' I have the impulse to keep crying 'I shall be late, I shall be late!' To think I ever suffered with insomnia!"*

Chapter Seven

Sheep Notes

"If you take care of the ewes, the ewes will take care of you."—Diary, 1924

A bunch of sheep is perhaps more suggestive of peace and serenity than any other animal prop that can be added to a landscape. The plaintive cry of a lamb intent on finding its mother, the ewes reassuring answer, the tinkle of sheep bells, add a musical accompaniment to the picture. When one looks at a bunch of sheep grazing peacefully on a meadow, however, he does not see the background which has produced this effect—of lambing ewes, slimy little lambs; of the summer heat, dust and mosquitoes; of deep snow and storms in winter; of predatory animals; of irate neighbors when the sheep get out of bounds; of mortgage notes to be met; of the hundred and one things that produce that seemingly peaceful prospect.

There is nothing that can take the place of experience in handling sheep. I mean the sort of active experience that comes from lambing, shearing, following sheep on the range, doctoring them, evaluating pasture and weather conditions, and the many other factors for the good of the flock.

I never go to bed at night without being a little bit thankful that I do not have to stumble out into the dark to look after lambing ewes—or, a strange paradox, a little bit unthankful that I am no longer able to run sheep. In the time that I ran them, the sheep taught me a great deal, especially about the sense of values, values of time. I came to feel that a day free of the sheep, must be carefully portioned and used.

Raising sheep is the oldest ranch business in the history of man. From the days when Abel tended his flocks to these days of soaring prices, sheep have been and continue to be the best live-stock investment for the man of small means.

I believe a woman has a better chance to succeed with a small bunch of sheep than a man. Little lambs are essentially like babies —caring for them is a woman's job. When a lamb is first born, he cares so little about living that he may lie down and die to avoid the job of living. He dies with a minimum of effort. He's here today and gone tomorrow.

During the first few hours of a lamb's life, his eyes and legs are weak, his tail is a lump appendage of no use whatever. He is wet, cold and very hungry. Why an all wise Providence could not have nurtured a little lamb, as are little chicks and other small creatures, for some hours after birth has always been a trying mystery to me. If he doesn't eat within a half day, at most, his troubles are over.

As always, just before lambing, one's feeling is that if one baby is a handful, a whole flock of babies is a riot that completely demoralizes your sense of security. Young lambs do not "stay put" like human babies. When one works his way into a badger hole, disappearing completely, there is only a faint cry to guide one. It is a bad job for several people shovelling frantically to effect a rescue in time to save him from suffocation. They may stick their heads in woven wire fences and choke, or strangle for no reason whatever; or they may develop some obscure disease or ailment that puzzles even a good vet. He may wander off into the wild blue yonder, and none of this bothers the ewe until the next feeding time. At best, a lamb's days are short and full of trouble.

There seems to be no regular system or order about the work with sheep, no matter how carefully you may plan. There is no push button method or system to lambing a bunch of ewes. Automation is no threat in our business. Each successive lambing tests the ingenuity and experience of the oldest lambing hand, provided the lambs are saved and a good percent obtained. Greeks are particularly good lambing hands. The story is told locally of brothers, young Greeks, who went into their lambing season rosy and rotund, but finished "lean as greyhounds." They always had a good lamb crop.

There are times when sheep truly try a person's soul. I am reminded of the man near Craig who committed suicide. He left a note which merely said: "It was the sheep."

Fortunately I did not make my venture into the sheep business until I had arrived at that stage of ranching at which one has acquired some appreciation of difficulties of any undertaking with livestock. Otherwise, the celerity with which an old ewe can lie down and die would certainly have been a considerable shock.

Theories about sheep fade like mist. You live in a fog of the best thing to do and find it is the wrong thing. Conditions vary with locality and climate. There is not much chance to succeed in a hit or miss fashion and there is very little element of luck. There is a rich reward and satisfaction for perseverance and determination.

Thoughtfulness and close observation are very important and I believe a person must like sheep to succeed. When people are unduly irritated by the vagaries of the flock's wanderings; when they expect sheep to follow the pattern of any other animal in the world except another sheep, then I know those people will never be happy with sheep, nor the sheep with them.

I am reminded of a cow-man who once stood near a little bunch of my gentlest ewes who literally liked no one but me. He said as he walked closer to them and intently observed them, "I hate 'em." My dander rose. "They hate you, too," I replied. He was startled. "How do you know," he asked? "Well, look how they are looking at you! "Damned if they don't look hostile," he said. An old sheep man once said to me, "You naturally like 'em or you don't like 'em. And when you quit smelling 'em, you know you really belong."

Sheep are creatures of habit and I think crowd-psychology affects sheep more than other animals, runs through them like a streak of lightning. A sheep cannot stand solitude or segregation.

A sudden hail storm can throw the sheep into complete pandemonium, and it is necessary to follow them and try to quiet them. If I am able to give them a sense of security, they will show patience in riding out the storm.

Unfortunately there are problems in sheep ranching other

than attending to the animals. Each year one has the difficulty of raising and keeping enough hay to carry them through the long winter, as reflected in my diary of March 1, 1932, when I wrote rather incoherently:

"*People are running short of hay. I have 69 tons, besides hay in the barn, perhaps a little more than enough to run through. This must be apparent for some of the neighbors who are short are insistent. They are desperate. One of those times when life and even friends are demanding. But a person cannot take chances. We may have bad storms yet. The ewes cannot be shorted. I have a somewhat spoiled stack of hay that I let three neighbors divide among themselves, with no charge, with the result that it aroused strife of a rare order among them and created considerable enmity toward me. Even a fourth man came in and said petulantly that he would have paid me a good price for the old hay. He indicated that I had not treated him right. He thought I was a friend. I could see that he considered me quixotic to the point of foolishness to have given the hay to the others. So my bread cast on the waters turned very sour!*

Last night one of the neighbors was back again in hopes of more hay. Perhaps I showed I was tired. She said, 'Well, all the work you do comes out of your bones.' Maybe she is right—my bones are very tired tonight, or as of the prophet: 'There is a great weariness in my bones, which at times like this extends to my spirit'."

My diary reflects that my difficulties extended through April. Winter can last a long time in the mountains of northwestern Colorado. The following is my entry for April 30:

"*Fourth day of bad storm. 10 degrees below zero. Snow deep. So tired that my mind refuses to grasp reality beyond a certain point. Trouble and difficulties almost cease to distress one after a certain point is reached, the saturation point, so to speak. Reality ceases to be reality and merges into unreality. Then one's sensibilities become numbed by too heavy a load of adverse conditions — the spring break-up, the restlessness of the sheep, the confusion of getting ready for lambing, along with the regular routine of feeding and watching the sheep. I know that any ewe could lamb any minute at this time, day or night, notwithstanding the fact that lambs are not due for several weeks. There's always a chance to save a 'premie' if one is on hand. The constant pressure of work, when one longs for a little rest and leisure, when one longs for still waters and green pastures, makes life seem to be rushing on one in a torrent."*

Time after time I have had to feel my way along with the sheep, always hoping that they would give me a "breather" from the constant day-to-day, minute-to-minute work. On one occasion, in 1924, I did get a few months enforced breather. Times got so hard that I had to take a job teaching school to earn cash to meet the mortgage payments on the ranch. During this emergency interval, I left a tenant helper on the place, caring for the sheep under my supervision.

Obtaining suitable helpers with the sheep has been a major problem over the years, often a trial and error affair. There have been a few pleasant surprises.

A Navajo smudge once raised my opinion of a very humble man to the nth degree. We were fighting a battle with the mosquitoes at the sheep camp. The herder was a nondescript, negative person in both appearance and behavior, but he astonished me one morning by appearing with a syrup bucket hung on a stick. From this bucket rose an acrid smelling black smudge, caused by a handful of burning or smoldering sage brush. He had put a few live coals on the sage brush, then swung the bucket around to create a draft. He kept this going in an arc about his head, and was thus in an aura completely free of mosquitoes, wherever he went. It was a heartening thing to see that little spiral of smoke out on the sage flats and know that someone could stay with the sheep. I began to observe the young fellow closely after that.

The only sheep I kept at the ranch house were "the bums," as the orphan lambs were called in sheep parlance. They needed special care and I needed them. At the homestead they had been given their bottles of heated milk before we left the cabin, and then they followed the bunch, never very far ahead of me, however. I am sure they looked on me as just another old ewe. They were an engaging and endearing group, gamboling along the trail, playing and jumping, appreciative to a degree, the gentlest of all pets, for that is what they grew into.

Guests never ceased to admire "the bums" and many times I was called upon to explain why they were called "the bums." As little lambs they could not find their mothers or a milk supply, so they "bummed" milk by feeding from a ewe available or one that would allow it. When the ewe's lamb began to nurse its mother, the orphan lamb—"the bum"—rushed in and joined the repast! The bums had a little pasture fenced near the house, and at feeding time let me know with loud ba-aas that they were receptive to bottles of warm milk. As I had ceased to milk cows during the hurdy-gurdy of homesteading, I now bought several milk goats. The goat's milk is the most digestible of all milk and almost a complete replica of ewe's milk. The antics of the goats and lambs were a continual source of entertainment to all comers, especially children. One little boy from town arrived at the ranch with his grandfather to see the goats milked, and his expectations were fulfilled to the fullest when each doe goat jumped up on the table in turn to be milked.

As grown ewes, the former "bums" never seemed to forget the care they had received and were often leaders, cooperative and usually obedient.

Outstanding incidents have come with flashing unexpectedness —the little lamb sucking a doe, for instance. The lamb, lost and wandering, had run into a gentle doe that had doubtless lost her fawn.

In winter the feeding of the sheep must go on. Jim, the homesteader who helped me, electrified me one morning by saying that in a day or so he was going "outside" for a while, which meant that I would have to get other help. This was a two-fold disaster, as Jim only worked part time and I did not have the funds to pay regular steady help. There was actually no one to get in this rather isolated valley.

We fed with the old-fashioned set-up, a team of horses. So the next morning I got up early, to make a stab at harnessing the team, my first such effort. I was very proud when Jim walked into the barn and saw the team all harnessed. I noticed, however, an abashed puzzlement when he looked at the team. He did not smile, for which I was glad. "It would be all right, Missus, only you've got both lines inside, between the horses, instead of outside. They wouldn't guide very well," and he quietly changed the horses without further·comment. Never again did I hear of the incident, which would have been relished by many in the countryside. Anyway, I gave Jim credit for being one of nature's noblemen for his restraint.

I went with him that morning, as I usually did, but this time with an awareness of the whole proceeding that knew no bounds. There was about a foot of snow on the meadow, where the sheep were fed, but the feed lot was packed like a pavement. The process of feeding was to make a sort of rectangular circle, throwing the hay onto the clean snow and gradually widening out the feed lot. This gave the sheep exercise and fertilized the meadow evenly. Jim tied the lines up to the standard of the sled and the horses, with their native instinct, followed the trail around as he pitched the hay.

The following day I was on my own, and although my actions were quite deliberate, I did harness the team correctly and my horses and I followed the same pattern of scattering the hay, with pride and relief. I then opened the gate and watched the sheep run onto the feed lot. No longer need I be a mere waiter at the gate and take consolation from Milton: "They also serve who stand at the gate and wait!"

The feeding of the sheep from then on for the next two years became routine, until the sheep increased to where more help was necessary. But in those two years the routine was often broken by vicissitudes that made it far from boring. For instance, the horse question became acute. Our original team had been all right for Dick, a good horseman, but for me they were virtually a menace. Skip, the sorrel mare, was highstrung to a dangerous degree, and the other mare had the misfortune to break her leg coming down the mountainside, so she had to be shot. This left me with only Skip, and my feeling of despair turned to desperation.

There was on the place a little, chunky saddle-horse, called Powder, very slow and somewhat lazy, his only gait being a hard, rocky trot. With a great deal of rearranging of harness, I "hooked"

Powder in with Skip. They looked very funny and Skip was furious. Horses never like to change mates anyway, and I am sure Skip would have run, but Powder stood firm. He thought he was tied as he felt the weight back of him, and he refused to budge. I felt completely whipped, as I stood on the load of hay, holding the lines. A neighbor passed, and after making a slight adjustment in the traces, he gave the parting observation that "the horses didn't match very good". I struggled through that day with the mis-matched team, and then borrowed a gentle old mare to work for her winter's feed.

The snow deepened that winter to several feet. My new hay haul was now across a river bridge, along a lane, and across another stretch of meadow. I had broken this meadow stretch by driving "the loose team," as they called it, back and forth, until a trail was broken, then driving the empty sled over it, before the load was put on the hay stack. However, all horses are not trail-wise and one morning, when I turned into the meadow, there was no sign of a trail. Perhaps I was no more trail-wise than the team. I could feel the sled settling down into the deep snow and I was standing to my ankles on top of the sled, with the horses unable to budge the load. Added to this, the wind was blowing a gale, and the snow drifting so I could scarcely see the team.

I was wet through and felt as though my clothes were freezing on me. While wading around trying to get the team "unhooked," I heard the faint rattle of sled chains and harness, and a man from up the valley pulled in with four horses. He helped me get the team back on the trail, and remarked that it was no day for man or beast to be out, much less a woman, and that I had better get to the house if I could find it.

You may feel a sense of overpowering obligation at such an incident, but Westerners do such things as though it is all in a day's work. They leave you with a pent up feeling of gratitude almost beyond expression.

And so one makes friends gradually for a lifetime, through the countryside.

Chapter Eight

Expanding

*"When good luck comes your way, push it! Promote it!
Believe in it!"—Diary, 1926*

My range rights for the flock were on government range
formerly devoted to cattle. To reach the range I had to cross a
neighbor's homestead which lay in between. This neighbor, a
bachelor, only homesteaded intermittently and was so unsettled
that I knew he was in danger of losing his 169 acres entirely. He
had given me permission to move the sheep across his land and
one day he suggested that I ought to buy his homestead, or what
he called "the relinquishment" of same. I actually held my breath
for fear I would rock the boat. I could think of nothing I wanted
more than that piece of land. The sheep had increased until I
desperately needed it; and I wanted the right of way to the range.
The man was naturally loquacious and my silence was actually
a goad. He hastened to say he would sell the homestead rights
for $500. I accepted. It was a phenomenal piece of luck and al-
though I did not have the money, I had no misgivings about
raising it.

This 169 acres, to which I refer as the "Long Place," was
natural sheep pasture—a sort of wild meadow grass with diversi-
fied vegetation of wild flowers, weeds, and peavines that the
sheep relish. There was also sage and service brush, groves of
quaking aspen, a flat threaded by a wild mountain stream, shaded
by deep and beautiful willows, with pines farther up on the ridge.
On a ridge near the cabin a whole grove of wild choke cherries
thrived—adrift with white blossoms in the spring. This was a
place of pure enchantment. The sheep must have sensed this as
they so often "shaded up" there at noon.

Aside from the natural resources, the homestead boasted a good cabin of rough pine boards, sturdily built and with necessary furniture—a big old kitchen cooking range, a bureau, bed, table and kitchen chairs. Just outside the cabin door was a spring of purest mountain water, several feet deep. I rocked up and fenced the spring to prevent a sheep or a lamb from falling in.

The grove of beautiful, quaking aspen near the cabin was the loveliest I have ever seen. With their birch-like white trunks and their heart-shaped leaves answering the slightest breeze, they have always seemed more living and human than other trees. The sheep bedded in those "quakers" at night and were contented to such a degree that the howl of coyotes seldom disturbed them.

A short distance away was another spring—sulphur water— that spread out over a flat surface into irridescent colors. Here the deer and the elk came to drink as they seemed to relish the water.

The seller reminded me of the unfulfilled government requirements for maturing title—that of living on it three months of the year for three years. By then, of course, I knew from experience about homesteading.

I rearranged my affairs by employing a boy to stay at the ranch and attend to the chores, so I could undertake my second homesteading operation. I would live on the new homestead for the three summer months when I would want to graze the sheep. With my good saddle horse, I was able to make the two mile trip back to the ranch to check up almost daily.

During late summer, when haying time approached, I was in something of a squeeze. I had to put my old horse drawn machinery in order, set in food supplies and hire a cook to prepare meals for the crew until I could be back to do the cooking. I would bring the sheep back to the ranch when my three months homestead residence expired and when enough hay meadow had been cut to provide pasture on the cut-over area.

Whereas, my first homesteading operation on the mountain side in front of the original ranch was challenging, this new homesteading operation seemed a Herculean undertaking, along with my now expanded sheep herd and haying enterprise. A friend, who operated the general store and sold supplies to many sheep outfits, told me my operation was too extensive for one woman. He said I was spread too thin. Finally he told me, "You can't make it." By this time, however, I had the bull by the horns, with no hope of letting loose.

I had to round up a hay crew and what a book could be written about that! A hay crew is never amalgamated, and usually consists of five or six men that have never worked together, each with a different idea about how the job should be done. This would make little difference with a good, stiff man as boss, but for me it took all the tact, diplomacy and sleight of hand that I could muster. Many times I felt like a juggler with three balls.

One day I rode out into the meadow just in time to see a fist fight on top of the haystack and I did not have the presence of mind to quickly turn and ride back to the house. When Tom, one of the fighters, came in that night, he did have the grace to say he hated that fight on my account, and by this time I had toughened up sufficiently to say, "I hoped you and George would kill each other!"

Another time, I went out into the meadow just as two young fellows were near the topping-out process, finishing a stack of hay. The stack was leaning dangerously and I suggested that it might be a good idea to top it at once. The boys ignored my suggestion and kept putting on more and more hay. They had scarcely gotten off the stack when it crashed down with a roar, and became a huge pile of inert matter that would take hours to re-stack. Never have I seen two more chastened boys that night at supper. I cooked for the hay crew, and we ate on a wide back porch that looked out onto the singing river. It was a pleasant place for hungry men, but the tension was high that evening. They waited in vain for me to say something about the upset stack.

There was much for me to learn about haying, aside from the personnel problems. If the grass went into the stack damp, it would be mouldy, and white mould caused ewes to lose their unborn lambs. If the hay lay on the ground too long, bleaching caused the loss of chlorophyl, the green element that supplies the stock with Vitamin A in winter. If the weather was bad we virtually lost the bet and just did the best we could do to save some hay.

It was always a relief after a season's haying operation to get back to the sheep. They started at dawn, leaving the bedground about four-thirty in the morning, grazing gently at first, then faster, as they got nearer better grazing. I was always glad of that early respite, of riding quietly along, watching the fading of the morning star, the soft, dusky light of the fading dawn as the reflected light of the sun behind the ridge grew stronger with a portent of the coming day, almost like a presence. The exhilarating mountain air always seemed charged with oxygen. One's spirits lifted, to have a new day, an unwritten sheet to be filled with the language of nature. For a time the problems and frustrations would seem very far away and I could almost touch the hem of truth. During such periods one involuntarily creates within one's self a cloister of memories, a reservoir for times when the spirit seems stale and arid and for moments of crisis.

A serious crisis did develop during my second year of proving up the new homestead. The Federal Forest officials decreed that my sheep range should be moved to what was known as the Sand Mountain territory, more than seven miles away from any of my land. I protested, but the Forest Office stated that my range was really in cattle bounds, and that there was sheep range available in the Sand Mountain country.

It was a staggering blow as concerned the sheep and their care. The area to which we would be moved was rugged, heavily timbered and parts of it almost inaccessible. Camp grounds had to be found where water was plentiful, not easy when I knew so little of that part of the country. I would have to look for an experienced herder to stay with them, since I could not keep in touch with the work at the ranch if I elected to stay with the sheep. A fifteen mile horseback ride for me each day was out of the question.

It seemed terrifying to throw the 800 ewes and yearlings into unknown territory with a strange herder; for, by this time, I knew all the pitfalls. There would be lost sheep, coyotes preying on the lambs, bears in that remote country, and always the work of moving camp at regular intervals as demanded by the grazing officials to keep from depleting the range grass.

Casting about for a herder I decided to try a Mexican; and, through a sheepman, I found Manuel. The sheepman told me Manuel was experienced but lazy. I decided to bet on the experience which I felt I must have. I knew that the range allotted to me was the last piece left in the sheep territory, and that it was almost too rugged for actual use. Manuel took over as herder, and we made the long move to the Sand Mountain territory. My misgivings about the whole deal at this time were colossal. It was more than the financial angle that worried me. I missed the care of the herd.

I was eager to commence the harvesting of the hay as soon as possible, so that the sheep could be brought down to the cut-over hay meadows. Manuel, lonely and anxious to get back to his wife in New Mexico, seemed indifferent and irresponsible to me when I had last been up to check on the sheep. The pressure from worry about the sheep mounted. This anxiety, coupled with another approaching season of haying, became almost insurmountable. I decided, finally, that I must find out about conditions at the sheep camp before we began the several weeks arduous task of haying.

With some trepidation, I saddled my horse, Headlight, early one morning and started for the sheep camp, seven miles away. I was gambling on locating the camp on the range which was moved every few days.

As on many other occasions during tense experiences in ranching, nature and the elements seemed to come to my side. I had not ridden far on the trail that mid-summer morning before its spell literally enveloped me. The trail followed a water course, partly natural and partly irrigation, but very steep. It then branched off into little groves of quaking aspens carpeted with exquisite wild ferns. At intervals there were beds of columbine growing in the dappled shade, and wild roses in a riot of bloom in the open sunny spots.

The little singing mountain stream paralleled the trail up and up into the cathedral stillness of the deep pines, with their fragrant incense, and became enmeshed in a chain of beaver dams, an intricate and interesting piece of engineering. Just above the mirror-like pools of the beaver dams, the stream seemed to have found its source in a deep, clear pool or spring.

I had heard Manuel, the herder, speak of this place and I knew I was near camp. I loitered a few moments having a drink, watering Headlight, and taking in the beauty of the spot. All the rush, vexation and strain had for the time being, been forgotten. I knew now what a friend had meant in a letter a few days before. He had said he wished he could get "out in your part of the country and follow a mountain trail." An executive of a big city bank, he wanted, for a while at least, to exchange his responsibilities for the simplicity and healing balm of a mountain trail.

As I crossed and recrossed the sparkling, gurgling mountain stream, I remembered having read that a spring comes from the heart of the mountain. I followed the stream on up through the aspens and pines. There were vistas of breathtaking beauty toward the valley below, and toward the mountains and the foothills beyond. I loitered a moment from time to time to drink in the beauty of it all. Unconsciously my spirits lifted as though I had put down my anxieties at the foot of the trail.

As I neared the camp I could hear the liquid Spanish of the men's voices. Another herder was visiting Manuel from a camp near by, and they were building a fire to prepare dinner. Manuel, without a word, reached for the Dutch Oven, then he said, "Biscuits, Mrs?"I replied, "Yes, and strawberries and cream!"—which I had tied into a saddle pouch. Their eyes glowed with appreciation. I never saw Manuel smile. He was a lithe, good looking young Mexican, with the mournful eyes of a lonely dog, but he did at times show appreciation.

On my last trip to camp, I had brought a book catalog with me and told him to pick out several books written in Spanish. These books had come. When I handed Manuel the books, the visiting herder's eyes stretched in wonder, and the books were almost rent in twain as they both grabbed for them. They both began to read from the same book loudly in Spanish, evidently a grandstand play to show their ability to read. When I persuaded them to take separate books, they continued to read loudly. The books Manuel had chosen were the Bible and The Life of Theodore Roosevelt. But their voices seemed almost to lull me to sleep as I lay down under the pines on a horse blanket a little distance away.

When I awoke I could hear sheep bells in the distance, and both herders were gone. I stretched luxuriously, refreshed and rested, with the fragrance of the pines, the tinkle of the sheep bells and the ripple of the little stream. I hated to move and break the spell. Near me lay a scrap of newspaper torn from some package brought into camp. I reached for it idly, then read it. I sat up then and read it again and again. It was part of a poem, the title and author's name torn off. I was quite moved by its message. It was to me a direct answer to all the doubts, fears and anxieties that had assailed me before I had started up the trail—the lack of courage, the negations, the indecision I had felt about the whole project of the sheep:

> *"When I quail at the snow on the uplands,*
> *When I crawl from the glare of the sun,*
> *When the trails that are lone invite me not,*
> *And the half way lamps allure,*
> *Oh, purge me in Thy primal fires and fling*
> *me on my way!*
>
> *When the wine has all ebbed from an April,*
> *When the Autumn of life forgets*
> *The call and lure of the widening West,*
> *And the wind in the straining rope,*
> *Oh, on the anvil of Thy wrath, remake me,*
> *God, that day!"*

I put the scrap of paper in my pocket and have moved it every year since to each new year book or diary.

The sheep were coming into the background slowly, in small bunches. They lay down content and replete, chewing their cuds. Manuel came in with the larger bunch a little later and began hanging out gunny sacks and lanterns in the bushes and trees to scare off the coyotes.

"I'm going to stay and see them bedded down," I said to him. But Manuel shook his head ominously. "It gets very dark and trail very rough—seven gates to find with all the drift fence gates—might miss them and then what? You walk miles—lost."

I was reluctant to heed his warning. The spell of the mountains held me—pure mountain magic! I strolled about looking at the lambs and ewes, now completely reassured as to the condition of the sheep, and also in Manuel's sense of responsibility as he went about busily building a few smudge fires. Then, as he kept shaking his head and hanging out lanterns on the trees, showing more and more concern as twilight deepened, I drank a hasty cup of coffee, ate a couple of Dutch Oven cold biscuits, and started down the mountain. At the top of the trail I turned and looked back. The camp was a picture of peace, the ewes and lambs bedded down under the pines, the smoldering camp fire, the pungent sweetness of the smudge fires, the glowing lanterns, the summer twilight like a benediction over all.

It seemed that we scarcely started down the trail when darkness settled down like a thick dark blanket. I had no idea it would be this dark. Fortunately my dog, Duchess, took the trail right in front of Headlight. I could see just that blotch of white in front of me. Headlight was not a good trail horse, but I assured myself that he was young and sure-footed. If it had not been for Duchess in front of him, I doubt if he would have followed the trail. As someone has said, "Only when the way is dark do the eternal verities shine out." This, I told myself firmly, was the same beautiful trail I had come over in the morning. I went on more confidently to the next gate. Duchess was already there and Headlight was impatient to get through. The trail broadened after the third gate, and at the fourth, I began to see the ranch lights—"the half-way lamp allure," I thought.

From then on my spirits lightened. We galloped on the open road after the last gate, all eager to be home. Home, I thought —it had a new meaning unshrouded by doubts as to the ultimate outcome of the venture. As I thought of the bedded sheep, of Manuel's interest and efficiency, I relaxed.

Chapter Nine

Difficulties and Illusions

> *"In common with other dreamers, I believe I'm tired because I don't like being hustled about and continually being waked up by realities—fairly jolted into action, bombarded by actualities when I am perfectly happy with impressions. I don't mind being bodily tired out but I hate the weariness of spirit that goes with it. To find life bearable we have to cherish a few illusions and dreams."*
> —Diary: Oct. 17, 1927.

There have been periods of intense difficulty stretched along the trail of my efforts at ranching, and yes, even of living.

"The better people think you are, the better you are likely to become," writes Somerset Maugham. Very true, and it takes a very rare order of courage to regain your self esteem and self respect and the esteem and respect of your fellows when you know they doubt you and look askance at your motives. Any highly sensitized person can feel the criticism of his fellows long before he hears it.

There were years in my life when I struggled without one word of commendation from any human being. Work! No one worked harder than I did during those years. I worked every day for years without one day off. It would have been easier to bear if people had not all seemed to have the same inevitable comment: "It isn't worth it". But it was those years that put the iron into my soul for the greater struggle that came later—the depression.

Frequently, when I was beginning to work my way out of

one hole, I would be confronted with a new wave of annoyances: a ewe refusing to claim her lambs, a lamb cutting his leg badly, the cows getting away, the mail sack not arriving—all causing extra steps. Vitality would again be sapped, frustration would set in at my inability to plan against such events.

When faced with an impenetrable forest of work, I would try to tell myself that there was no approach but to drop a tangent from a star—no way to run a line except to hope and believe and keep on working. On such good days I would feel about my work as did the old Negro woman about her religion. She said: "I wears my religion like a loose garment."

On other days, the work would become a hair shirt. People who have never worked hard physically can have no idea of the utter weariness of hard work, of the longing for leisure. Just as people who have never been short of money can never quite realize the desperate straits of trying to live on "nothing a year". Sometimes I think that you have to be hungry or cold, or not have the price of a postage stamp, to develop a real sense of values: My old diaries reflect periods of severe discouragement. For instance:

> "I often seriously wonder why I was put on this earth. I am totally unfitted for most of the things I've undertaken —almost crushed at times with my own sense of ineptness in practical things. There seems nothing worthwhile in my make-up except appreciation. It is like trying to make something with only one ingredient—just appreciation."

I have always longed for immunity from irritation, for a gracious and leisurely life with time to think and feel. Instead of that, most of the time I was hustled along with a taste of this and a glance at that and never time to enjoy things. If one could only simplify existence, if there were any way to live more graciously! I believe that is what money would mean to me—to buy a little time or leisure which is actually necessary to one's spiritual well-being. Toil doesn't corrode nor stultify up to a certain point. Work, hard work, is very good for a person; but drudgery that drains away one's forces stops spiritual growth. I believe it would reduce one to a spiritual dwarf, in time. The business of making a living hustles one about so, and often kills illusions so ruth-lessly.

Making a living is not easy for a man, but for a woman it can be real tough. Often she feels like she is thrown to the wolves. She is less able to keep abreast of things by sidewalk or nail keg talk, and she must hire more help than a man. She is often charged higher wages, and the business woman can be the prey of the ne'er do well. She must constantly fight against a tendency to be soft, and there is always prejudice. The following plea is from an early diary:

> *"Please do not let me use physical disabilities as an excuse, nor the fact that I am a woman, but let me remember I am a woman in a man's place; that I must have the guts of a man and the patience of a woman."*

Financial burdens, particularly, weary one's mind and spirit almost beyond endurance. Notes at the bank always had a way of coming due! When a person takes over a small equity in a ranch and works to pay it out, he has about as much freedom as a plantation Negro. Indispensible things weigh one down to such a degree that there is little room left for an uplifting item. One ranch woman said to me: "I don't even want a geranium. I just want to shut the door and walk out!"

One great consolation, however, during my straits—I could always go to my diary and write to myself:

> *"Give up if you must, but not without a struggle. That is running up the white flag. Perhaps the thing you are search-ing for is within your reach; so never listen to the voice of discouragement, either from within or without. The one from within is most dangerous. There is a way out of every material difficulty. If not, there is an alternative, and if not that, there is a compromise."*

At another time, an old diary shows that, as a tonic to myself, I wrote down my predominant characteristics that might be con-sidered assets that I should try to build on to meet my difficulties: "dogged determination; individuality to the nth degree; love of solitude; analytical thinking; desire for harmony; habit of reading; liking for animals and nature."

My diary reminds me that during the struggles, I had my better moments:

> *"Then, when you've toiled and struggled and sweated with your head down and your back bowed, suddenly you get a vision—a vista. Truly, 'without vision, the people perish.' Recently I went to bed so worried, confused by business and a multitude of things to be done—mountains of difficulties literally. After tossing for 15 or 20 minutes, I tried to get mental control by staying on the same thought train: that a real faith can move mountains. Then, the negative flash that told me that mountains could not be moved by faith; but the Bible said so and so it must be—the mountains of doubt and discord and difficulties that could be moved by faith and have been."*

One is interested to take these flashbacks, to recall my other means of release and relief. During another period I find the following in my diary:

> *"I have been trying lately to think of myself as working for someone else at this job and find it stimulates and gives me a different outlook. I am very thankful to be able to be out of doors, to work by myself and as the very old say, 'to have my faculties'. I am often driven and wish I had time to live more graciously. But I suppose one can cultivate poise in business as well as in social life. One thing I know: I have passed another milepost. I have quit being lonesome. I stop and wonder about it sometimes and have the same reaction I have had in realizing that I am recovering from an illness—a sense of restfulness and peace with yet the memory of what lies so immediately behind me."*

In a life once made almost desolate by death and disillusionment, I had struggled toward a light, just as most others struggle, I presume. The desire for peace of mind was so intense that I was determined to have it. I decided that I must be like a traveller or adventurer getting ready for a hazardous journey. I would strip my life of all impediments, superficialities, artificialities—and put sincerity in place of these. I wanted to seek the star of truth. But how difficult I found those plans for execution!

While undergoing difficulties, they often seem intricate and ponderous, but upon looking back they shrink to their rightful proportions. I remember an unintended detour I once took, while worried, off a trail in the snow. Some animal might have made it in a playful mood.

Then, there have been my illusions, and a sizeable chapter on my life could be devoted to illusions. For instance, even after successfully finishing a hard project, like paying out a piece of land, there would sometimes come over me a terrible sense of futility, a reaction, I suppose. The feeling of accomplishment has a way of falling short of what was expected. I have worked hard to develop a philosophy about illusions.

Like the old maid who said she would never be happy until she quit struggling, perhaps I shall never be entirely happy until my illusions are all destroyed. Yet I agonize over the smashing of each one. Life takes a terrible toll of people who cherish them. I started with a large stock.

"Ye shall know the truth. . ."—so, in my better moments, I believe I had rather know than to be sheltered and protected. One should be free of prejudice, cowardice, superstitions; free to meet life as a cooler, harder, crisper person, who looks life squarely in the face as it really is.

The point of view, in this matter of illusions, makes a big difference. So many of us judge by our own standards. We lug our own background in, and it obscures our point of view. I once knew a Southern woman, reared with all the "refinements," and she judged us western provincials by those standards. She wanted to chop wood, but was under the impressions that it would be offensive, especially to men. But, after a long time, she was unshackled. One day, finally, she philosophized to me: "All men are pretty much alike. They don't mind their women doing hard work if no one is looking!" I knew this was a little nosegay on the grave of her illusions. She was a happier woman swinging that axe than she had ever been waiting for some man to swing it.

It is a shock to find that a friend has qualities that make us shudder when we accidentally stumble onto them. I lost a friend the other day—worse than death. He did a thing I cannot forget. He was cruel to a weakling. Time after time I suspected, but this instance proved it beyond a doubt. Being cruel to a weakling is the greatest of all cowardice.

Some people seem to have been born without illusions. They are the cold-blooded, hard-fisted people, who see things exactly as they are. They are the statisticians of the world, and are usually more successful. They have a natural insight into character. They know the human heart can be wicked, and so their friends do not disappoint them.

As for the illusionists, they stumble along with their heads in the clouds and their feet not too securely on the ground. Occasionally they touch the edge of a cloud, or they catch the exact color of a rainbow. If they are commonplace illusionists, like farmers or ranchers, they may merely lift their faces to feel a mist of rain, or stretch out their hands to a west wind or feel the intense beauty of a snowy woodland. They actually feel abstract beauty, these people with illusions, and they hate to part with them unless they can change some tiny part of this abstract beauty for the concrete. Their creative instinct is seeking expressions—a woodland brook, a bridge, a picture, a poem, a perfectly equipped and managed ranch, things hewn from abstract into concrete beauty.

Actual things have grown from the cherishing of dreams and illusions, yet we are prone to smash the illusions of others. We pity people who cannot see through things. We have lost a measure of faith ourselves and other people's trusting faith irritates us. "All religion is superstition," an Englishman said to me at age eighteen, and I gasped—a terrible shock, a blinding-crashing.

Sometimes a beautiful, vital monument of service springs up from broken illusions. I know a woman who resolved, after every illusion of love and friendship was destroyed, to come back to life through service to her neighborhood of phlegmatic, toil-ridden people. She had no illusions about that. She did not expect appreciation, but she saw their need. There was no ostentation. Her right hand knew not . . . her means were limited. She was already overworked, but the opportunities for service came, a social service of a glorified order.

One conclusion I feel certain about: that there is no escape from difficulties and shattered illusions; and the only way to deal with them is by building up a reserve of understanding and complete honesty of purpose, unswerving faith in one's self to do the right thing, and to use this as a bulwark or a citadel.

Chapter Ten

Tender Episodes

"A single light way off on the mountainside, a will o' the wisp inviting the imagination"—Diary, 1927

ONE SUNNY AFTERNOON

I rode up into the hills to see an old woman who was blind; a deathbed repentance on my part, I should have gone sooner.

She was pitifully glad to "see" me. Her parchment-like hands clung to mine as I gave her a box of candy I had happened to pick up casually as I left the ranch. She asked me to describe the box —she felt the frilly paper cups around the pieces of candy. With a tightened throat, I tried to answer. "God put it into your heart to bring me this!" she cried over and over. As I realized the pleasure this careless afterthought gift gave her, I felt a soul-searing humility. Why hadn't I been to see her sooner and more often? Why hadn't I thought of her more frequently in that dark world in which she lived? Why and why and why?—I bitterly asked myself as I rode back down the trail. Do I have to learn and earn my soul's salvation in such stumbling, blundering ways, like a child learning to walk—my soul's salvation, which, in simple terms, is only thoughtfulness and kindness to those around me!

I sat in the room a few weeks later, the room from which she was buried, with a little group of neighbors. Again there came back to me the relentless sense of humility I had felt that other afternoon when I had taken her the candy. She had given me something so deep and lasting that the memory will always remain. As I rode back down the trail, I thought of the beautiful words attributed to Stephen Grallet: "I shall pass through this world but once. . . . ."

*　　*　　*

WISHING FOR A TEA WAGON

The honey-dew was thick on the undergrowth, giving it a glossy, varnished look. The flowers were the loveliest I had ever seen—mariposa lily, blue flax, blue bell, gentian, Indian pinks, wild geranium and wild rose. Further along the trail these gave place to thimble berries, with their broad leaves and starry white blossoms. Then a turn in the trail brought me into a grove of "Quakers" sheltering wild ferns that grew as high as my stirrups. Incredibly beautiful they were, shimmering in the shadows of the quaking aspens.

I found Gasper's camp in a deep grove of pines. "It is like a house," I said to him, as I gazed up to the patch of blue sky visible above the spires of the pines. "But it leaks," Gasper replied, with an unexpected sense of humor.

Later we fried our chicken in the Dutch Oven and the two Mexicans visited us. It was nice to eat quietly and not to have to take part in the conversation. I felt like a good quiet child, eating my dinner and taking no part in what these wiser brown people were saying. After dinner I felt even more a child when Gasper brought out his Story of the Bible to show me—a highly colored and plentifully illustrated book. It was delightful to read the Spanish from the pictures.

Later I slept in the teepee and when I awakened, the world seemed very far away—a place of vexations from which I had escaped and released to this, temporarily at least. Even the so-called creature comforts seemed of no importance. The place was complete—two teepee tents, one to shelter supplies, the other to sleep in; a camp fire of pitch with a gypsy-like tripod of quaker poles, from which a wire was suspended to hold the Dutch Oven directly over the flame. I was glad Gasper cooked on a roaring glowing fire like this. The nearest pine boughs were scorched slightly and the scent of them, with the appetizing odor of outdoor cooking made one ravenous as animals must be at feeding time. I had only instincts. Again and again I wondered why one must be so hampered with things when life can be so simple. Enough could be packed on two horses for me to live in kingly comfort.

"Tea or coffee?" Gasper asked abruptly and I answered, "Tea." Even as I answered, I remembered civilization's latest effete baby, a thing to be dressed up in the proper linens, silver and china, to be coddled with dainties and rolled around before company. It occurred to me that I should never again want a tea wagon—that thereafter it would seem a bit foolish to me. Doubtless there will be times in the future when I shall dress up and find myself doing all that is proper in the atmosphere of tea wagons, but I doubt that I shall ever again take a tea wagon very seriously.

* * *

CHAIN REACTION

I came in contact with something very real this morning. A great deal has been written about smiling. Stereotyped things, like "Smile, damn you!", always make me feel morose, but if you will smile one genuine smile early in the morning, the returns are consequent. A telephone girl smiled at me over the wire, literally miles of smiles, and as I opened the door to a tourist a few minutes later, he got the reflection of her smile. Although I had declared war on fishing tourists, I smiled and said, "Yes, catch as many as you can." Then, the smile became a laughing chorus as they followed the stream into the meadow—one smile that had spread from the town twenty miles away, to my lower meadow. The most intangible things are the most real.

* * *

A SCRAP OF PAPER

The snowshoe rabbit is one of God's most beautiful creatures. As he runs through the deep snow, his angular frame has a marvelous grace, but I had never had a close look at one.

One night, about midnight, when I was living in a cabin in the hills, I heard a thumping in the snow and a mysterious rattle of paper. I got the lantern and there, just outside the door, was a big white rabbit with a piece of brown paper in his mouth. He did not seem particularly startled, but hopped back of the cabin, still holding the piece of paper in his mouth. I was puzzled and followed. Three times we went around the cabin before he disappeared.

The next day I was visited by a good friend, the neighboring cow puncher who had helped me in many a pinch. "What were you doing with a light going around and around the cabin last night?" he asked. "Following a rabbit, like Alice," I replied, "but he must have gone back through the looking glass. I lost him. He had a piece of brown paper in his mouth. I had never seen a beautiful rabbit carrying a piece of paper in his mouth at midnight, so naturally I was interested. It aroused my imagination and gave me insight into how Alice must have felt when she followed the rabbit."

"What was he doing with a piece of paper in his mouth?" asked the cowpuncher, skeptically.

"That's what I was trying to find out. Perhaps in the council of rabbits, as of diplomatic circles, 'it was just a scrap of paper'," I replied.

The cowpuncher rode on, shaking his head over the idiosyncrasies of town people who move to the country, and I went back into the cabin wondering at the omniscience of a neighborhood where you can't walk around your house at midnight without arousing the curiosity of your neighbors.

Some years later I received word that my old cowpuncher friend was ill and I went to his bedside. After some reminiscing, my good friend said, "I have liked you, but I never understood you."

"Nor do I," I answered fervently.

Then the whispering voice: "Would you say a little prayer," he asked? I was nonplussed for the moment, then I said, "Yes, the most beautiful of all prayers." I stood beside the bed and repeated "The Lord's Prayer."

Then he asked, "Who was Alice?" A wave of humility swept over me, thinking of my perversity and teasing. I told him the story of Alice. "So she did live back of a looking glass," he said. "Wish'd I'd read it," he continued. "You wouldn't have cared for it. You have to grow up with it. You have to be a lonely little girl," was my reply.

"I'm going now," I said, but impulsively I reached over, took one of his work worn hands in mine, then leaned over and kissed him on the forehead. "I'll be back again," I said. "I may not be here," he said, with a flash of his wry irony.

My eyes were misted over and my throat constricted as I found my way down the rough, steep stairs. I was glad there was no one below. I stepped out onto the porch, high above the ground, and looked at what seemed a view of all creation, a section of the

Great Continental Divide, always changing with the seasons, yet never changing in the grandeur of its structure. Instinctively I relaxed as I stood there. Absolute beauty and absolute truth must be inter-related, I thought, and together they furnish consolation to release the most healing forces of the spirit.

The steadfastness of the mountain range gave a sense of enduring reality—a part of eternity, of the scheme of things.

*   *   *

"RIDING THE GRUB-LINE"

I had forgotten the expression until this old fellow came in, shabby, riding a little Texas pony. I could imagine him on the highway trying to dodge the traffic, he who once had lived on one of the largest ranches in the valley, now a derelict, old overalls and a T-shirt, patched boots. I remembered his spread of former days: saddle horses, good machinery, the trappings of cowboy royalty: chaps, spurs and bridles. It all came back as I looked at him sitting on the porch, thankful for a few minutes respite, reprieve before he wearily climbed back on the little "cayuse" and got back on the trail—a trail that, following the beaten path of a beaten man, led to nowhere! He had once been profane and very sure of himself. I had often been affronted by his profanity. Now his voice was muted and no offensive word escaped him. He reminded me of an old stray dog, seeking to beguile someone into a word of approbation or affection, to be noticed, to be wanted, to be needed.

I got up and prepared a quick meal. He ate with relish, seasoned with appreciation. I remembered what the hired man had said once under similar circumstances: "Pet a stray dog and he'll come back!"

"Alright," I thought, but this old man had once done me a great favor; he had furnished me a team when it meant saving hay with storm threatening. As he rode off he said, "I'll be back to see you next summer!"

*   *   *

MY SUMMER VISITORS FROM THE CITIES

The out-of-doors has come into its own, even farming and ranching. The ugly duckling has become a swan! The automobile is partly responsible, and the passing of the Victorian Age is more so. It is polite now-a-day to eat all you want and not be ashamed of it. It is popular to know how to do things. What chance has the girl in this day and age who cannot swim or ride horseback, or hunt or fish? The young lady who used to do water colors, or paint china, or embroider, is as obsolete as her works of art. It is a positive age, and even women are determined to do something worth while, especially when they are having a good time.

Traditionally, country people have felt that they were not quite as smart as city people, and some city people are quite willing for this impression to continue. In this era of communication, however, we are getting better acquainted and any misimpressions are going with the wind.

Country people are likely to make an effort to keep town people from seeing the seamy side. "You sleep late," I've heard myself saying, "and you don't get up until you're ready"; meanwhile planning that most of the work would be done before my guests appeared. But people seldom sleep late in the country. To begin with, they have probably slept well, after going to bed at a decently early hour.

In my house I have noticed that guests who sleep in a certain room invariably appear early, very early. That room has some intimate association with the dawn, for guests usually come down talking about the dawn. There is nothing distinctive about the room. The walls are papered in a rather faded gray paper; the furniture is simple white enamel; and the rug is one of bluish-gray grass; but the windows open to the east and south, and it is the corner room of a high second story. One could not possibly pull the shades down at night, for that would shut out the mountain air and so the dawn looks in and wakes you.

"It is much more beautiful than the sunset," one visitor said earnestly, "and it goes so much more quickly." She assured me further that she was going to get up earlier the next morning to be sure to see all of it.

A well-known surgeon, a man of high standing in his city, visited me not long ago, and I was somewhat overcome by the amount of data about my own section of the country that this man had acquired. We took a drive in his car, and all that he did not know, he expected me to know—the altitude of the mountains, the names of the trees, and shrubs, the location of points of interest, statistics, in fact, so many statistics. The next morning, he came downstairs before the breakfast fire was built. He spoke in his precise, technical way. "Have you ever noticed the star that sets just before dawn?" he asked with eagerness. "Or I suppose it sets. I've watched that star every morning now, for three mornings, and I've never been able to see just what does become of it. The dawn always gets me. I never saw a star just like it—or, maybe it's the juxtaposition of the mountain and the star and your pine tree."

"Blue spruce," I corrected, and hated myself for being literal, but the man scarcely heard me. He was seeing his dawn, and I was relieved to know that he didn't really care whether the tree was a spruce or a pine, and that he had one real impression to take away with him along with all of his statistics. Perhaps he had a great many more that I did not know about, for many people are as chary about speaking of impressions of beauty as they are in discussing the inner voice of their religion.

* * *

REINFORCEMENT

The very efficient typist in the government loan office had only one hand. Her attitude toward those who waited in the office was one of poise, unfailing courtesy and understanding. When she was ready to leave for the night, she dusted her typewriter with loving care, and straightened her desk to the last letter and paper. She exemplified Emerson's: "Do your work and you shall reinforce yourself."

Her quality reminded me of Francis Parkman, one of America's greatest early day historians, whose western experiences were embodied in "Prairie and Rocky Mountain Life." He could write only five minutes at a time, so great were his physical disabilities; yet his book is unsurpassed for grace and style, and is of first authority on early western lore. He lived with the Dakota Indians, and impaired both his health and eyesight in securing material for his writing. We are still reading his books today.

* * *

WORTHY OF THE SACRIFICE

No smallest luxury had been known by the woman whose funeral we attended soon after we came into the country. Her life had been one of privation and hardship, but she must have had many friends. The old log community house where the funeral was held was crowded.

A serious, young Episcopal minister conducted the services. In his surplice he had a spiritual, uplifted look; and as he spoke, he turned directly to the husband of the woman and their two children. They were a troubled, bewildered group. The husband had a far-away look, but the boy and girl, wistful youngsters in their early teens, appeared quite attentive. The minister dwelt briefly on their loss and bereavement, spoke of the mother's life of self-denial in a new, raw part of the country, of her hard work, of what she had sacrificed for them. Then, he turned even more directly to the little family and said simply: "May you be worthy of the sacrifice."

*   *   *

Chapter Eleven

Wayside Friends

"The privilege of catching glimpses of the furred and feathered friends of the wayside often comes at the most unexpected times."—Diary, 1928

At twilight, one night at the sheep camp, we were hunting the "bunch quitter," an old ewe that often failed to come in with the flock. If we did not find her, a coyote might, so all hands turned out to hunt her. As I worked up the side of the mountain, back of the camp, where the bunch quitter often stopped at a little spring for a late drink, I rested for a moment near a pile of brushwood, and saw a party of rabbits at play.

There were eight or nine rabbits of assorted sizes, from little bunnies to old jacks, jumping and playing with an ecstasy that was the poetry of motion. They did not see me, and I stood back of the brushwood watching them and feeling that I had been permitted to take a page direct from a fairy book. The moon came up over the ridge and the lighting was better. The rabbit game became wilder and wilder. It was the rhythm of movement incarnate. Their soft gray bodies were pliant and relaxed, their ears always erect, their eyes bright and eager. There was a fey gaiety about the game that surprised me. I had never thought of rabbits except as serious nomads of the brush and sage. What capital a Walt Disney would have made of such a scene. Even to my earthbound eyes, it was enchanting, magical!

Then the call came from the sheep camp. The bunch quitter was found, but I went back down the trail feeling that I had seen one of the secret things of the wild woods!

* * *

The strip of willows between the river and meadow throbs

with life, a veritable frontier for the small animals that live there. I observed one of these small creatures one day, from a clump of willows. Clad in vestments of royalty, an ermine coat, to be exact, he appeared to be dancing on the meadow. At first, I thought he was giving vent to a purely pagan dance of joy, or perhaps unconscious gratitude for the warm sunshine, the crisp autumn air, and the musical murmur of running water nearby. In reality, the ermine was engaged in the prosiac business of getting his dinner —catching field mice and bugs, then somewhat sluggish with the approach of winter.

In my eagerness for a closer view, he saw me. The dinner-dance ended, abruptly. He vanished, the very earth seeming to swallow him. He had disappeared into a hole about the size of a dollar. A few feet away was another hole, and some ten feet away, were three more. "The windows and doors of his house," I was thinking, when suddenly his head appeared through the very hole I was examining. Both of us were terrifically startled. He jerked down and I jerked up. Next he came out of one of the holes further on. Curiosity possessed him. His whole slender body was tense with interest, only his nose and whiskers twitched. His ears were pricked alertly forward, his eyes beadily bright with excitement. Nor was his interest greater than mine. I had never seen an ermine at such close range. We stood for a long minute staring at each other, before he again disappeared.

Back at the ranch, I consulted a natural history book for more about him. "An ermine or stoat," I read, and instantly rejected the "stoat" as gross and unsuitable! I read on, "The mustela erminea is a small animal of predacious habits"—but I read no more. The book would have gone on calling him hard names, but I knew other things about him. I knew, for instance, that he ate his meals dancing merrily on the greensward in the sunshine; that he slept his sleep, cozy and warm, in his mysterious subterranean house with three windows and two doors; that he ran with incredible swiftness over the snow in search of adventure; that in summer he changed his raiment of royalty for a sober brown coat, invaluable to an adventurer such as he. I knew, indeed, that all life was a gay adventure to him, his the joy of living untrammeled by a host of things that vex and encumber the spirit of man.

*   *   *

On a snow packed trail, I met the muskrat. Now a trail is a decisive place to begin a friendship. One must be either openly friendly, or he must turn tail and be done with the whole adventure. In the late spring in the mountains, trails are narrow with high banks of snow. I expected the muskrat to run, but to my surprise, he backed up against the side of the trail and appeared to raise a supplicating paw. Later I found his foreleg was injured and that he could not actually put it down. Regardless of my feminine dislike for any kind of rat, I took him back to the ranch and fixed him a box in a sunny window. He was a little fellow, not as large as a park squirrel. He ate almost anything I gave him, and drank or spilled a surprising quantity of water. But one day, when I was filling his drinking cup, I found he had been using the water for his bath. Stupid of me not to have known that he, who virtually lived in the water, would want his daily bath! He must have been very desperate on this day, for he stood directly under the stream as I poured the water into his cup. After this, his bath became a daily rite, with all in attendance who might be at the ranch. His coat improved and became sleek and glossy, beautiful in color, a clear, rich brown, shading to a silvery faun about his breast and stomach.

"His hide is worth seventy-five cents," he cowpuncher said one day.

"Would you actually rob the little furry Joseph of his coat, for a few paltry pieces of silver?" I asked.

The cowpuncher gave me an affronted stare. "He's only a varmint," he said, "and they are mean. His family likely threw him out of the nest for fighting. He might have bitten you except for your heavy gloves."

"I never heard of anyone being muskrat bitten," I defended.

Regardless of how he came by the wounded leg, it healed, and one day I took him back down the trail to the willows, leaving one side of the box open. The next day, when I went back, he was gone, but I felt sure that I had a friend in the muskrat village near the beaver dam.

*   *   *

The beaver dam appeared to be only a quiet pool, fringed with reeds, and encircled by willows. I little suspected at first the cross-section of wild life it harbored.

One day, as I sat quietly with the inertia of perfect content-ment, in the edge of the willows, near the little stream that fed the beaver dam, the drama of the beaver dam began to unfold. First, a small snake startled me by swimming past, evidently intent on making the dam on schedule, his head well up out of the water, alert, with an air of "going places." Next, a large beaver appeared on the surface of the dam, then submerged again, swimming swift-ly toward a conical structure of mud and sticks, his house, at the far edge of the dam and which I determined to examine later on. Suddenly, a muskrat scuttled out of the water quite near me, sat on his hind legs in the sunshine, appearing to dry his coat, nibbling at a green leaf which he expertly held in his paws and covertly watching me all the while. Almost at that same time, a school of tiny minnows swam into the little stream, miniature, silver gray fish, letting me examine them at my pleasure, swimming with a happy, flirting movement, entirely indifferent to the fact that they are the natural prey of the other sojourners of this world of water and reeds. Then, with a faint rustling in the willows, a big mallard duck launched herself gracefully into the water, her flock of little ducklings tumbling after her, performing antics that reminded me of little boys at the ol' swimmin' hole.

I had been so completely absorbed that I had not noticed the arrival of the kingfisher, but from the top of the willow, he had seen me. He gave his raucous alarm, and the dam was instantly devoid of life—a mirror of peace, reflecting the blue sky.

*   *   *

A colony of small birds live in the lilac bush beside my living room window. Snowbirds and little brown wrens are year-round residents, while blue-birds, robins, flickers and others visit the lilac bush in summer. The lilac bush is thirty-five years old, grows directly against the side of the house, and reaches the second story window, consequently it is an ideal site for bird apartments.

The nest building of these window-side friends is fascinating to watch. There is a definite strategy about bird life, if one has the chance to observe. These little birds build on boughs or branches that will hold their tiny nests, but that are not heavy enough to hold any of the prowlers, cats and others that might molest them. One marvels at their wisdom in choosing such a sanctuary, safe from marauders, and close against the house where storms do not rock their nests.

The ordered life of these small defenseless ones is truly amazing, living safely and happily as they do, under the heaviest odds, while·man, with his superior intelligence, lives in a state of frustration and stalemate, seeking greater and yet greater instruments of defense and destruction.

These small birds follow the rhythm of nature, the immutable laws that need no enforcement, the laws with which, if man could once get in harmony, would mean cosmic order instead of chaos.

As Elizabeth Barrett Browning wrote:

> "Oh, the little birds sang east, and the little
> birds sang west,
> And I smiled to think God's greatness flowed
> Around our incompleteness, around our restlessness,
> His nest."

*　　*　　*

Coyotes to most people, and especially ranchers, are anathema; picturesque perhaps, but outlaws nevertheless, and creatures to be despised and hunted. Nevertheless, one small, friendless, coyote once claimed my attention and protection.

In reality, he scarcely seemed a coyote when I first knew him, but more of a little brown puppy that longed for his wolfish mother. From the back of the den, he had seen her and his brothers and sisters killed. He had escaped only because he was more timid than the rest and had cowered in the darkness until the rancher's thirst for revenge was satisfied and the carnage was over. The rancher had put him in a box and dropped him on my front porch. He was all but starved when I found him, and after a few overtures, he accepted milk from a bottle. The day I was going to leave, the rancher said, morosely, "I don't know who's going to feed him after you leave."

"What did you intend to do with him in the first place?" I asked.

"There's a doctor in town asked me to get him one," answered the rancher. "Would you take him in?"

I joyfully assented to this.

The doctor received the coyote with the strange exhilaration that very tame people often entertain for very wild things. But I had misgivings. The coyote plainly mistrusted the doctor's every move.

When I saw the coyote again, my heart sank. He was not full grown, but he was a full-fledged coyote. To give him exercise, the doctor had fastened his chain to the clothesline, and as the chain slipped along the wire, the coyote ran back and forth all day, the spirit incarnate of restlessness. I felt his collar and found it too tight. As I passed the doctor later on the street, I mentioned this to him and he agreed that the collar needed changing. Toward evening, when the doctor took the collar off to enlarge it by punching another hole in the leather, the coyote was turned loose for a moment, and this was truly his moment out of all time. The grocer boy came in at that moment, leaving the gate open, and the coyote escaped to the low foothills beyond the doctor's house.

I was secretly glad, but now, when I hear the coyotes howling at night, and know of their depredations of sheepfold and farm flocks, I remember with misgivings that I once befriended one, helped nurture him, and directly helped him to escape.

* * *

Donald Duck is on his hummock in the river, assured and happy. His drab little partner, Dorothy, sits faithfully on her nest in the willows near by. They come about the seventh of April to the pool by the barn.

They come as surely as spring time, in fact, more surely, as spring is often delayed for a time. But Donald and Dorothy know the ice will be off the river in April, food supplies will be available and the security of creature comforts and their feathered routine lies ahead.

Dorothy finds a safe place on a little island, never entirely covered in high water and safe from polecats and weasels, while she lays her clutch of eggs. Donald stays nearby. In the interim of acquiring the proper number, they swim, duck and dive in the back water or eddy between the island and the river bank, which is my observation post. They have no fear of me. Evidently, to them, I am only another animal and quite harmless. So I see the whole process of creation.

* * *

Coming from wayside to the hearth, the depth of feeling for the four-footed friend is ever enhanced.

Our household animals do not have the saving grace of a sense of humor, nor need it! Man does not have instinct as do animals, though the woman-animal claims intuition, that twin sister of instinct! Animals have memory and intelligence, but they do not have intellect or reasoning power as does man. Are these the differences that set man apart from the other animals? Or does the difference, as one writer suggests, date back to the Garden of Eden, where animals were not tempted by the forbidden fruit, as was man, and so are not troubled by ideas of right and wrong? We sometimes wonder whether man's code of morals has any place in the animal kingdom. If animals are provided with the creature comforts, they usually pursue their way peacefully and happily.

One need not be a confirmed zoophile to enjoy animals. Little children delight in them, aged people find solace against loneliness in their chosen pets.

Walt Whitman loved animals and wrote of them:

"They do not sweat and whine about their condition,
They do not lie awake in the dark and weep for
their sins,
They do not make me sick discussing their duty to God,
Not one is dissatisfied, not one is demented with
the mania of owning things,
Not one kneels to another, nor to his kind that
lived thousands of years ago,
Not one is respectable or unhappy over the whole earth."

Chapter Twelve

Moments Of Reflection

> *"If every individual stopped every day for a few moments of sober reflection, what a different world this would be."*
>
> Diary, 1942

Commencing in the 1940s, after the ranching operation reached stability, with less likelihood of foreclosures, the diary comments became somewhat introspective. There is less writing about sheep increase, more about self improvement:

> *"Only in relaxation can I have real renewal. I must realize that any worthwhile creative work comes from relaxed slow growth.*
>
> *"There is already too much tension in the world; no need for me to add any. It causes illness within the person, ills between individuals, and tragic ills between segments of people, called nations."*

At the beginning of my diary for 1943, I wrote a "Program For the New Year":

> *"1. Believe in people, look for the best in them, and by all means avoid self-esteem; and accept constructive criticism in the right spirit. Give praise without stint; find something pleasant to mention so people will leave in a glow. You can praise the obvious talent, the flower of another's personality; or you can hunt out the little school of inspiration, modest as spring violets, that longs for light and encouragement. Warm them from the inside—this is a cold country. Reduce*

that debt of mistakes of other years by paying off in kindness this year. It will take some of us the rest of our lives to balance the books.

2. Sum yourself up, analyze. You must have some slight talent. Hunt it out and use it, polish it; at least it will add to your enjoyment. Take stock of yourself in relationship to last year. Was it a disappointment or did you advance 365 days worth? Then how many days if not 365? No one wants Christmas every day in the year, nor to be gorged with good resolutions, either; but if we could stand on the threshold of the New Year, and look back to the old as one of happy accomplishment and a sure foundation, then the New Year would be beautiful, uncharted country, waiting, rich in experience.

3. The genuine always carries a rare value stamp. Stereotyped axioms, flattery, none of these will do. Never brag or boast even by inference; and try effacing your own personality completely except in relationship to the personality of other people.

4. Don't get grudges and carry them around, pet and coddle them until they develop into full sized peculiarities.

5. Budget your time; don't overdo. If one task is heavy, try to lighten up the next one.

6. Never be smug, buoyant or noticeably tactful. Poise yourself; sit quietly, keep your voice down, and don't ask questions from curiosity.

7. You will get more agreeable or disagreeable as you get older. You cannot stay as you are. The tendency is to get less attractive. You should pay careful attention to details, personal. You can be a reasonably popular old person. You can be well informed, or moderately so. Even if you are sick, you can wield a certain influence. You may not be very smart, but you can use your native commonsense, even horses have that. No good merchant would put his worst goods in the show case, and his best on dark shelves, but I've often

*done just this—showing corroding criticism instead of na-
tiave kindness, for instance.*

*8. Don't try to avoid your originality, individuality, being
yourself. There are already mobs of people all doing the
same thing—houses alike, clothes alike, cats and dogs alike.*

*9. If you haven't enough character to have self control about
eating, your reserves of resistance are low, indeed. Remember
the man who compares you to a neighbor and says, 'She is
light on her feet.' Work is harder for you because you are
heavier. You have an objective, and that knowledge enriches
your whole being and personality. The longing for self expression, for better things, that was always in you, must have
meant something. Cherish it. You will largely work out your
own salvation, so make out a concrete program of do's and
don'ts. If you've been living on the negative side of life,
swing over to the positive."*

Emerson says: "I like the silent church before the service begins." Well, I like the silent morning before day completely breaks.
There is nothing like it here in the country. There is quite a long
period between the fading or setting of the morning star and the
rising of the sun. There is promise and peace at this hour that forti-
fies one for the later stress and turmoil the day may bring. "Pause
and reflect" is a practical slogan. It may save many blunders and
cul-de-sacs. After a pensive period I could write such thoughts as
the following:

*"Which of these people are you? The child undeveloped,
full of ambition and dreams, the girl unthinking, reaching
for life; or are you the young woman, busy, sure of herself,
important; or just the woman bewildered!*

*A composite of these? No wonder. They are unrelated.
They have only the same parentage or heritage name. No
wonder you don't understand yourself. No wonder you are
puzzling, groping for a solution."*

I look back now to that little girl on the gallery steps and
know how completely isolated and insulated she was. Few could

have penetrated the shell of loneliness that encased her. I can see her very clearly as she comes nearer to me through the years, always searching and reaching out for something that seemed beyond her grasp; elusive, impossible, but existent none the less:

"Again there is no escape. A scent, a sound, a strain of music, takes you firmly in hand and leads you back into the land of memories. It bids you to look again and remember. You are back in the room where your mother died. Again there sweeps over you astonished resentment, scarcely a consciousness of grief, only an over-powering sense of loss, a bewildered sense of hunting the way in a world where love had ceased to be—trying desperately to right this condition of a loveless world with ambition. Doing my best and always with the feeling that it could not be the best. Trying to stifle love with ambition; a pitiful effort, like a seed struggling toward the light.

Grief really stops only when we begin to forget, so in memory of those you love, grieve fully and completely. Something very precious has gone out of your life, buried, just so much faithfulness, loyalty, instant service and adaptability, love and gentleness—rare qualities that cannot be bought, that were never paid in proper measure. You must realize that even nostalgic memory—a sense of sadness—is better than a sense of futility."

During some moments of reflection, I wrote to myself about how to handle moods:

"For God's sake and for your own sake, walk! Walk until your troubles begin to weigh less heavily. A walk in the open may not help you directly to meet a note that is due, but it will make you sleep and eat—and it may surprise you with an inspiration. You may not believe in inspirations, but if you get out in the open country, where God dwells, you are more likely to meet them.

If we could only cultivate a good mood as assiduously as we do a bad one, if we never forgot a favor as we never forget an injury, what a difference it would make in our mental aura. Negroes cultivate moods, singing monotonously. Birds must sing themselves into happy moods, I think. Conversely, people work themselves into tempers. When it comes to our troubles, our own ego serves as a magnifying glass. Poise is merely a perfect balance of moods."

If we could adjust ourselves perfectly or nearly so to life, what would it mean to ourselves and everyone else! If we could temper ourselves to be strong enough, and yet remain pliable enough to understand! I believe half of one's difficulties would settle themselves. A machine in perfect order does the work; so it is with a person, perfectly adjusted in the white light of truth.

On balance, however, I doubt if any thinking or thoughtful person is really happy, could be completely happy. We may be stimulated by some event, of course, but I doubt a state of lasting happiness. Contentment, through the anodyne of work, makes life reasonably satisfactory, once we consign feelings of true happiness to the very young, the robins and kittens.

The best approach to contentment is not a struggle for money, fame or influence—but for control over our own emotions, aspirations, and the continual delicate adjustment of our own identity. That identity is a combination of heredity, environment and the spiritual spark of divinity (some call it conscience) that lies within all of us. The deep inner urge for the expression of identity cannot be escaped. It colors every action, affects the course of our lives.

One may not be conscious of it but, doubtless, each person evolves a philosophy. I never "came by things" the easy way. There are still times when it seems I must go through a morass of difficulties and doubt before I can say to myself, "You've evolved a philosophy—make it work."

Peace of mind seems to me the most desirable of all states. There are so many restless ones trying to scale the walls. It is a condition you reach entirely by your own efforts. No one can help you much.

The chief thing of importance is to face facts and decide what you are afraid of, what impedes you. Then follow this by constructive thinking of what you really want from life, followed by the pertinent question: Are you getting it? It may be material things; altruistic or abstract yearnings unsatisfied; or ambition ungratified. Looking at one's self objectively, however, thinking a subsequent course of action through, is a strenuous effort.

My diaries are almost a barrage of suggestions made to myself:

"You wake relaxed. Why? Because your mind has been completely free of problems, worries—unharried. So your body rests—why not carry over this plan into the day as much as possible. You control your mind, or could, or might."

"People are isolated by so many different things: wrath, ignorance, filth, bad habits. Spring is a good time to remove the isolation."

"Weakness is likely to attack you as success; so beware of that particularly terrible viper of self-righteousness, disguised as a silken covering."

"Strike a balance on the help, to demand enough but not too much, to take into consideration their limitations as well as your own."

"Never kill a dream—your own or anyone else's. Never shake someone's faith. The stuff that dreams are made of is durable material—the infinitesimal spark that may develop into a powerful force."

Fear weakens our ability to deal with difficulties. Most difficulties are transient. With faith, we can ride the storm or even the whirlwind; and going through it often gives us tranquility, assurance, and the experience we pocket. We may almost feel grateful for the experience.

The principle of truth underlies everything that is enduring and right; the fundamentals of truth are always simple. We recognize them almost intuitively. I know that I have been struggling toward this light as long as I can remember. This desire for truth is, perhaps, the only real talent that I have. It is the leaven that leaveneth the whole mixture. If one cleaves to the truth, seeks it and is guided by it, this attitude of mind and life is sure to lead one out of the "Slough of Despond." But this cleaving to the truth is not as simple as it sounds. We have all our own inhibitions and weaknesses to fight, or to disentangle. My diaries are a mirror of my inner struggles:

> *"There are as surely ghosts as there are broken faith, lack of duty done and lip service, to rise up and confront you when you least expect to remember such things. We pay for a keen sense of enjoyment with an equally keen sense of suffering. The highly sensitized individual has the widest range of emotions, the most points of contact."*

*   *   *

> *"So you've grown a little today, whether you're seventeen or seventy? You can feel the growing pains. You didn't 'flare up' and say things you would regret later. You were hurt, but you literally 'held your peace'. Think of that! You did not 'get even'."*

*   *   *

> *"No patient after a terrible operation recovers in a day. The first night is terrible. Tissues must mend and heal and so it is with great mental distress, and worst of all, there are relapses. If you have climbed out of a black pit, and survived, only to fall into another, must you remain here, spend your life like a slave in a dungeon?"*

*   *   *

> *"If, after all the terrible mistakes and disillusionment, you have found the way, well, there's some comfort in that. But remember, nothing but love counts as you get older; and we are as we are, God help us."*

*   *

> *"I believe 'Think things out' would be better than 'Think things over'. Actually, almost any difficulty can be thought out, or thought to the point of decision and action, if we persist. Indecision is a state of mental discomfort."*

*   *   *

> *"It is a psychological fact that when you have done a great deal for people, you take more from them than from others.*

In other words, you have invested yourself in them. After you have saved a person's life, you feel responsible for him. It is like buying stock on a margin."

Extended difficulties, hinted at above, have had some consolation. The memory of hard times has become so indented on my mind that only actual disasters of the major sort, such as illness, death of friends or relatives, can affect me for long at a time. Trifles can disturb one, but poise often comes by continual determined strife with what appears to be overwhelming odds, if one concentrates hard enough on eternal verities.

Fortunately, we have written aids, some beaten paths, in searching for truth, eternal verities. A big help to me has been "Imitation of Christ," by Thomas A. Kempis, a mystic. One thinks of this lonely monk in his cell searching his soul for the immortal truth, and feels the prodigality of spiritual devotion that must precede such a work as his. Out of the depth of his devotion came a religious book that, next to the Bible, has been read by more people than any other.

Eternal verities are as plainly discernible as the stars, but often seem as far away. If, after we discover eternal verities, we try to hem them in, to bridle and drive them, we are appalled. Changes of growth are definite parts of the eternal. When someone asks me if I believe this or that, I long to say: "I believe it or not, as the case may be, now, today, but I may not believe tomorrow. What I believe then may be entirely different."

At one point, in my quest, I wrote:

" 'As the hart panteth after the water brook—a living God.' Not the God of orthodox religion, not the God of isms and creeds, but a living God, a God who will fit into the scheme of everyday life, a God somewhere in reach of the finite mind."

At first, a person who has had companionship is very lonely. But, as time goes on, solitude becomes a habit and people really encroach on one's consciousness. The out-of-doors helps more to overcome loneliness than anything, together with the "wild and woolly ones" and the company of the horse and dog.

In working with others, we use some of our capacities; in working alone, we are likely to use all of our resources and draw on our reserves. Working alone develops self-reliance, concentration and foresight.

Justice Holmes once said to Harvard students: "Only when you have worked alone, when you have felt around you a black gulf of solitude more isolating than that which surrounds the dying man, and in hope and despair have trusted to your own unshaken will—then only will you have achieved!"

Living alone affects one's sense of values. It makes one overestimate the joy of independence and under-estimate the pleasure of contact with other people. It can give one contentment and self-reliance. It cultivates sensitiveness, but it can also cultivate selfishness, as pointed up in a dairy entry:

> "Nothing can discourage you as much as the hurt you have done to another—even a thoughtless oversight, a sin of omission, so to speak. I protested once to a friend that doing a certain favor for an acquaintance meant considerable inconvenience to me; and my friend's wise reply was, 'Not nearly as much as the help you give means to him." In other words, it hurt me very little, but helped him very much. I learned a lesson."

And then later I wrote:

> "There are so many people who need sympathy or more than sympathy—compassion. I think Christ must have had the feeling that all these sorrowful ones were reaching out to Him when He gave Himself and was lifted up on the cross. The only way to plumb the depth of suffering is to suffer with people or in like measure. Lifted up through suffering —there was no other way to pay that debt. If I had to choose between a capacity for understanding of either happiness or sorrow, I believe I would choose sorrow in the light of experience."

Some years ago I wrote a summation to myself:

> *"As we reach middle age, we begin to realize that the objects of youth have somehow eluded us. Perhaps our ideas or ideals have changed, or perhaps our plans have failed to carry. But as we have gone along the way, character has been formed. In the struggle for self expression, certain characteristics have developed. And regardless of conditions or circumstances, these characteristics, amalgamated with understanding, produce a human being definitely useful in the scheme of everyday life. Just the qualities we already have, if mixed liberally with kindness, can result in a fairly decent person. Maybe we can still do something worth while. The harvest season may be ahead."*

Chapter Thirteen

Mellow Days

"An all-pervading sense of peace tonight—not a sound except the sheep bells, the occasional cry of a lamb, or the night talk of the robins."—Diary, 1940

A home, a beautiful valley, books—life at the fullest and best. The evening star, a glimpse of the aurora, grand and perfect moments, when one becomes a part of the great design and feels the potentialities of life stirring within. Also, there are homey, lesser moments, for the exercise of some of those simple tasks and talents—making a nut fit a log screw, or using a roller shade for a cupboard door. Why should I be singled out for all this?

It isn't given to many women to have such happiness, such a sense of realities—to start off with the sheep at dawn, wild rose columbines, lunch beside a stream. The years have gone by like a dream.

Love of the land—someday I must write more of the deep, sweet peace of the place; the lovely familiar contour of the hills, the stars so close and friendly, the murmur of the river. There are some places so tranquil and serene that one feels that God must not be very far away.

No music ever made by an instrument is as sweet as that of rippling water; no painter's brush has ever caught the prodigality of color that nature flings across the hills in autumn; no scent is as agreeable as new mown meadow hay or dying leaves in autumn; no author has or ever will catch the full import of a mother's love or loss; no one can ever tell in more words of the actual glory of the morning star. These things you have to live with to know them.

They are written only in the book of nature. They are the genuine on which so-called art is founded.

Over in Chanute Gulch, a place that belies its name, there is a small gurgling rocky stream, among pines and aspens. I had the good fortune to see humming birds building their nest. The nest was a thing of rare beauty, a tiny, carefully constructed bit of workmanship formed of leaves, hair, twigs, carefully lined with sheep's wool and feathers, cunningly fastened securely to a bough in the willows. I watched the mother bird as she brooded her eggs, then both birds as they tended their young—little fledglings not larger than a thimble. There were anxious times when a little red fox prowled under the tree or a magpie threatened; but finally the flight of the fledglings and the empty nest.

> *"Birds and animals largely regulate their lives by weather conditions, I suppose. I noticed the sheep stopped eating in the early afternoon and stood quietly as though enjoying it, since the forenoon had been very warm. Your spiritual barometer rises—the sky gray and misting rain, the air soft and moist as a baby's kiss!"*

One cannot walk in the country and remain a pessimist. I doubt if one can intimately know nature and remain an unbeliever. All of the recent hue and cry over a famous naturalist announcing that he is an atheist went over my head. The very strength of his negations proclaim his faith. Personally, I am never alarmed by the statement of a nature lover or worker who says, "I do not believe in God." He has merely acquired a poise and communication with nature that makes God and nature seem one.

One reason people enjoy contemplating nature, as Emerson says, is because they feel themselves identified for a time with the great design.

A man stopped at the door not long ago and asked to fish. "But I don't really want to fish", he said, "I just want to get down on the stream and sort of rest and be out of doors." I asked him what his business was and he answered somewhat wearily, "We manufacture check books."

The next fisherman had a more hurried and harried air. He walked up and down, waved his arms, and rumpled his hair as he talked. "We have only an hour or so to fish," he said, "and we want to see the Grand Canyon before we get back to Los Angeles." He mentioned the Grand Canyon as though it were a picture show in town.

When one takes time in contemplating nature, one tends to become philosophical. In my small notebook which I carried when it was just the sheep, me and nature, I made many observations:

> "*The strange talk of nature will become a part of your life if your being is attuned to it.*"
> "*Nature never disappoints. Human nature does. There are hurts, but suffering carries its own anodyne. In moments of terrific stress one's sensibilities become numbed. Later on as this merciful anesthetic leaves, suffering begins but with it comes a certain courage and strength.*"

* * *

> "*True wisdom is said to be compounded of knowledge of God, plus knowledge of self. A soul searing experience leaves scars, but we can try to ignore the scars and profit by the mistake.*"

> "*Descartes says: 'Nothing is wholly in our power except our thoughts.' These same thoughts can cause us to conquer our strongest adversary—ourselves! If we can approach a problem and as Descartes says, 'divide its difficulties into parts, as many as possible, and examine them separately and carefully, it might help toward a solution.' All of which is only a simple thinking through of our problem. No battle was ever won by hastily plunging into combat and beginning to fight. Plans must be drawn, preparations must be made, to win a campaign.*"

* * *

> "*I remember the day a complete stranger brought me a fine sheep dog. I remember the day a man came to my door during a shortage of help. Truly, no one knoweth what a day may bring forth!*"

* * *

> "*Home is the place you love—where your heart is, where you find peace and contentment. If added to that you also*

have independence and can attain a measure of happiness, that home is your Heaven on earth."

Most of my diary writings are directed only to myself, in the nature of fight-talks. However, at times I note that I became quite expansive and varied:

"Well, think of sheep grazing, or apple blossoms, or of rats in an empty barn. Did you ever stop to think when you are worrying about things, about how few items we need in life to be happy, I mean the elemental needs. All on one pack horse—oh, yes! your son or daughter, but maybe their chief need is to share your burden. Remember you are not God."

* * *

"Standards to be kept. Ah- dear me!—forget your standards of the pretense variety and be natural and easy."

* * *

"Remember always that life is kaleidoscopic. Everything changes. Take advantage of opportunities as they arise. This may be the high moment. 'Like a tree by the river of waters'."

* * *

"Say what you please—if a woman can make a man laugh, she has him. It is equivalent to making him comfortable since the reaction of a laugh is mental comfort."

* * *

"I like weather to be like chilled wine, with a little tang to it. Weather can be too equable. It takes a little alloy to make a good metal—or character—or weather."

There has been a reluctance on my part to become all-business, since when business becomes a part of one's everyday outlook, it is likely to obscure one's vision as to sheer beauty. Business sense insists that the thing in question must be marketable and negotiable, whereas much beauty has no trademark or price tag.

I found out that in the business world a novice learns slowly, painfully and sometimes at heavy cost. It took me years to learn the value of compromise. An impasse or a deadlock can be broken often by a middle course, or, if dealing with what is known as a "hard trader," by giving in somewhat to his demands.

In any event, I put on a show every now and then, for protection. One old man, known for his shrewdness, offered a cow for sale. I was timid and felt at a disadvantage. I feigned toughness and said, "What's the matter with her?"

On the other hand, about the same time as the above crusty event, I write such thoughts as the following when alone with nature:

> *"It pays real dividends to put the right books in the hands of children. My first memory of which I am conscious is of hearing my mother read 'The Cricket on the Hearth' aloud to me. The lamplit room in front of an old fireplace was indeed a perfect setting for the reading of it. Much of it I did not understand, but the impression of that lamplit room, of the family so closely united about the fireplace, is one of the most precious memories of my life."*

Freud says: "To be completely honest with one's self is the very best effort a human being can make," and thereby he wrote his meaning of the cure of the soul—psychoanalysis.

The above I found out for myself the hard way, through solitude and hard work, work actually far beyond my actual capabilities or knowledge, the results of which still astonish me, and even back in my middle age I wrote:

> *"Life does such funny things to us. It takes a little girl, shy and timid to a pathetic degree; and, with no preparation faces her some 35 years later with a set of conditions that would cause the strongest man to flinch and take stock of himself. Looking back from middle age to the little girl on the threshold of life, the change that has taken place during the interval between childhood and womanhood does not seem a growth. It seems an amazing transition. It makes all the little insignificant happenings of those years seem suddenly significant in effecting this change."*

Thoreau's exemplification of simplicity has helped me greatly —just to refuse to follow the crowd or to try to "keep up a front," to consistently cast off the unneccessary in every way. When my boat seemed about to sink, I just unloaded some of the cargo. If I couldn't find the money to pay a herder, I herded the sheep. If I couldn't pay a hay pitcher to feed them in winter, I pitched the hay. I learned so much, for instance, how to break open a stack of hay, with the top hard frozen with ice and snow, that must be shovelled and then chopped open with an axe.

During this grueling process, the great reward was that I learned to depend upon myself, to develop my own resources, to believe in myself, to evolve a sense of values.

Working with the sheep brought out unexpectedly my strongest characteristic, i.e., that of a zoophile, a lover of animals. I should add that the gentlest, most appealing and helpless of all animals naturally appeal to one's highest instincts of protectiveness and care.

Not long ago I walked down from the winter camp where the sheep were being wintered. An experienced stockman bought an interest in the bunch of sheep; and with the sheep under his intelligent care during the winter feeding season, I found my dream of leisure at least partly true.

After 45 years continuous work on the ranch, I finally took some time off, and now I heartily aver that everyone should have a vacation. There are many reasons.

A complete change of scene widens one's horizon and keeps a person from becoming insular.

It relieves the sense of responsibility that becomes almost a dementia if one does not break the chain occasionally.

A person's ego and spiritual forces are renewed. One receives a different point of view, often an inspirational one, as of the feeling that I will go home and do this or do that thing that I have always wanted to do, but which I have put off doing.

A vacation gives us a relaxed attitude that we cannot get when locked in the goose step of our usual routine—the lawn must be mowed, the fence must be fixed, the bills must be paid and all the endless chain of things that gall and bind us in routine.

Lastly, the pay-off, the best part of a vacation—the trip home, the arrival there, our friends, the dear familiar contour of the hills of home, the rustle of the trees and the ripple of the river. We have left our old battle-scarred ego far behind us and can face up to life with more zest and vigor. And, as the "darkies" in the South say, on their return from a trip "Maybe we feel just a little bit journey proud."

During my vacation, I recorded some observations:

"The Grand Canyon gives one a profound inspirational feeling. Standing at the rim, looking out across its awe-inspiring stupendous beauty, a person is held enthralled. The spectacle seems just too large and grand for the mind to grasp fully. Added to this, the immediate surroundings are beautiful. The Bright Angel Lodge, with its sequestered little cabins scattered through the trees, has not been exploited, but managed with restraint and imagination. There were no concessions nor blatant advertising—only a sense of remoteness and grandeur."

"At the Indian Reservation, I did not see the poverty and perhaps squalor of the Indians, but I did see their simplicity, which most of us do not possess in this day of speed madness: the little spotted dog standing at the edge of the road in happy confidence, a group of little Indian boys with bikes and dogs in a vacant desert lot. A game of sorts was in progress. The 'dobe houses and the old cars—places directly on the edge of reality; so that if you opened the adobe shacks or houses, you were looking at a far horizon. The houses were rather far apart. There was a feeling of space and peace in consequence. The roads were rather dusty, dirty, with only a few cars, little traffic. No sense of urgency or speed—only the peace of the desert. I felt it deeply, and relaxed."

Chapter Fourteen

Time, Precious Time

"Trying to fight old age is like playing to break a gambling bank. All we can do is to stay in the game, but we know the cards are against us."—Diary, 1961

"Hold Back the Dawn" is the lovely, imaginative title for a story I once read. If one could only hold back the years! Just when a person has reached a stage where experience, appreciation and sensitivity help, then the burden of the years settles down. Time suddenly assumes a great significance.

The theory of life being only a fragment of eternity does not prevent us from cherishing time. If we are living our best, each day comes to us fraught with interest and zest. The feeling that "anything can happen," and often does, gives a rare savor—a fresh day that can help to spell success or failure by the way we use our God-given time. What a challenge this makes of each day! In some respects, we older people who have some mission still unfulfilled, some hobby, some keen interest in life, are the happiest of all people. There is more time to enjoy people—little children, young people, their interests in school, business, friends—and our contemporaries with connotations of the past. There is time for little courtesies, letters, for reflection, all those things which the busier years crowded out. There is a release from many of the things that have bothered us in our younger years. Old age can be like the end of a beautiful day—the peace of dusk, like a benediction.

Age brings wisdom, clarifies vision, gives us at last a sense of direction. We see ourselves objectively. Except for mere physical comforts and security, one's wants become very simple. Appreciation of abstract things grows. A new book, or magazine, is concretely entertaining—things that appeal to our mental side mean more. Both the magnitude and the miniature of nature mean more. Older people can be happy even under the most adverse circumstances, if they want to be. We may not be able to do what we want to do. The whole pattern of life may change or be incomplete, but we adjust ourselves. We may lose those who are the nearest and dearest, but we can go forward courageously.

Youth is too close to the passing scene, too enmeshed in it to get the full savor of events. If we could only have the vision of age with the forces of youth! There is a gulf between age and youth that is indeed difficult to bridge. The aged desire to be understood, and youth's passionate desire is not to be thwarted. Old age is more tolerant than youth as to the mistakes of our forebears and of those around us. Even the successful aged have tested failure at one time or another.

Old people, however, like old plants and trees, are likely to become critically root-bound, by staying in one place too long; and root-bound plants, whether human or vegetable, are difficult to transplant. The only answer seems to be to move before it is too late. Even though we do not like the move, or the location as well, it widens our horizon, gives us a different perspective.

We must constantly combat a feeling of creeping inadequacy. When I feel myself slipping, I think of Dickens' story, or book, "Barnaby Rudge," of that half-witted boy's raven, or crow, which knew virtually only one sentence: "Never say die!" When Barnaby was tormented, beaten, abused and confused in the riots, the raven always perched on his shoulder and cried, "Never say die!" My diaries, of late, reveal my moods and entreaties:

"We must pay a terrific price when we go against the forces of nature, either material, physical, mental or spiritual. Nature demands value received."

* * *

"The Smith place was deserted. I stood there thinking that on this place people had struggled, loved and hated, feared and hoped; and the futility of life engulfed me. The place was forlorn and deserted. It had been so full of life once, a

sort of crossroads of endeavor. Waves of nostalgia! But life goes on. We cannot stand still. We must face things and go forward courageously or turn backwards like cowards and retreat."

"I do not want to be like the old fellow, when interviewed as to the secret of his long life, replied, 'Why, I just kept on breathin.' There is so much to do and time so fleeting. Time goes so fast that I have the sensation of buttonholing each day and asking it if it is the 11th of November, or the 12th, or the 13th, as the case may be."

*   *   *

"I am really not an old person—not a cell in my body is the same. I am a new person. While I have lost the pristine glory of youth, my identity remains and I don't want to be anybody else. Remember Goethe's Faust, at 80—Churchill, Baruch, and Grandma Moses and her paintings."

*   *   *

"Youth is like spring, age like winter. If only we could die as nature does, like a leaf letting go from the branch in a pageant of beauty—a final flare up of life before the silence of winter."

"The inertia of approaching age is absolutely deadly and must be fought even as dragons are fought in fairy tales. Mr. W. called me in to see Mrs. W. this morning. She has heart attacks. She was frightened and blue. They talked of getting a doctor, but what she really wanted was sympathy and reassurance. She had the usual fear of old age, like the rest of us."

*   *   *

"I find I have to believe in myself more as I get older, much more than I ever have before."

*   *   *

"Don't be plain spoken. Try to think ahead, and 'play it cool'."

"Spiritually hold fast to faith—faith in others, in ourselves, and read The Ten Commandments once in a while."

As you get older you do not tip your hand, but hold it close to your shirt front. You hope the next deal may be better. You have the feeling of gratitude that at least you are still in the game. After all, as of the time-honored cliche, it is an achievement to play a poor hand well. And there are people all around us who are doing just that without complaint.

When time is so limited, one can have a conflict of desires. A lover of books wants time alone, to read and to re-read, to commune with the best of minds, while there is time. On the other hand, one wants to do some worth while acts of service, as stated in the following petition from my 1960 diary:

> *"As time gets shorter, give me understanding; keep me placid, calm, and sweet. Help me to try to do some good with no thought of return or thanks. May I remember that when we embark on the great adventure, all we can take with us are the things born of love and kindness, and all worth while that we can leave are things of the same sort— not 'things' at all, but elongations of personality."*

The doctor said, without the bat of an eye, that he was not sure whether my heart trouble was coronary or angina. I confess to a sinking sensation. "If you live right, you may live your time out." Certain dietary instructions followed, a prescription to dilate the arteries of the heart. Only by pressure had I succeeded in getting this diagnosis. At the previous visit, he had said, as he removed the stethoscope from my chest, that my heart was regular; but now the cardiogram told the story.

"Any emotional strain will be bad for you", he continued, "and above all things, don't worry."

Don't worry, I thought. I came home, tired, depressed, whipped and frightened, but as I walked into the living room, I felt a surge of reassurance. The lovely room with its books, piano, typewriter, flowers, seemed almost human with its greeting. I stumbled through the ranch chores, thankful that I had them to do.

Next morning, fresh even after a fitful night's sleep, I took a careful survey of my affairs. I realized it would make a complete change in my way of life. Always a margin of time must be allowed on any project—no rushing.

I must guard against any undue pressure—no arguments. I must learn to rest before I become tired. I must never push myself as I had been doing.

Slowly I must set my house in order. Decisions must be made as to property—as to the future. I must re-evaluate the things necessary to do, as essential from the things entirely inconsequential.

This last changed my plans completely as to the immediate future. What use to add a utility room? Or to re-survey a fence line?

After the survey of my affairs, my heart lightened. Decisions were easy to make. I had little choice. The inevitable is never pleasant to face, but it can be faced with equability, if no physical pain is involved.

Strangely, I found in the weeks that followed that I had time enough for what I had to do.

The status quo of my life was completely changed. I was going to live by the minute or day, instead of by the month or year. As when leaving a dear friend or place, I ceased to be critical or analytical. Future plans were simplified. What was essential to my well being, or useless, answered the question. Worries diminished. I was unhurried. I planned to the minutest detail for the immediate future, so I could avoid stress, tension and strain. I do not raise my blood pressure by any argument.

When I stepped out that next morning, this was all in my mind. The mountain air seemed like a huge oxygen tent. I was thankful again for the routine chores. The dear familiar contour of the hills seemed to enwrap me in peace. Only those who have lived out of doors can know. The sound of the river—everything had a new, special meaning. Standing there on the steps for just a moment, time seemed to stand still and deep appreciation caught up with me.

I had been rushing through life. Now, perhaps, on nearing the threshold of the last Great Adventure, I was given this reprieve to savor the beauty, the meaning and understanding of things all around me, to go meet it "not like a galley slave."

There were things I had always wanted to do. With the elimination of non-essentials, I find I have time enough at least to start them. Maybe I'll get some of them finished.

Life can be beautiful to the hurting point, if this sort of hurt does not leave scars. Even though you may have heart trouble, of the acute sort, it pays to take stock. The spirit may be forever young, even though the body machinery threatens to play out. Lots of good work has been done with faulty machinery. Lots of old machinery is standing in fence corners that could be used. Lots of people have given up who could still be useful.

Recently, I wrote in my diary:

"Perhaps all we can do is to keep our sail right, like a mariner, to catch the prevailing breeze when it does come."

Old age is like a benediction if one has a sense of accomplishment through self-expression. As the sunset is often the most beautiful part of the day, so nearing the end of life is often the most beautiful part of life.

I often think of the sheep, and the ranch as a sanctuary, filled with memories. I often feel that I must have been in a place like this in some former existence, I so instantly become oriented in the surroundings. We have a better understanding of events as the circle of life begins to close. Looking back gives us perspective.

We have acquired a lore of connotations that make contact easy with almost anyone we meet. Life has become very peaceful and its savor very sweet.

The sunset may last only a little while and the night comes, but who can doubt that the night is followed by dawn and another day!

Chapter Fifteen

Passing In Review

"There is no greater, more simple means of following our objective than keeping a diary, though it may be only a record of small events and a few thoughts. It gives us a sense of order and continuity".—Diary, 1954

1896

During my class period on Morals: The teacher watches me like a hawk after a chicken, eyeing me all day long, and I have not been doing a thing. It is enough to make anybody want to be mean. It is a heap more fun to write this than study. Max went to the office for not knowing his lessons.

*   *   *

Dick and I had a big row on the porch about Culbertson, the silver question and so forth. I do not think he (Culbertson) is nearly so cute as another silver man I know.

*   *   *

My grades today, and all good marks. Had a horrid music lesson in "Les Marguerites". Am writing this on Delphine's back. Bob has intellect not.

1897

Two parties today. Dick and I went to Mrs. P.'s, a kid affair, and had fun. They played "Goodnight" and "Please and Displeased". They sent us from the room to promenade, but we just went on over to the other party to see how it was coming on. It rained and I got my velvet and chiffon all damp and bad.

*   *   *

affairs, the better. A good listener is always in demand. Others like to talk about their own affairs.

1915

On the place (Steamboat Springs Ranch) two weeks today. Dick branded calves. There are 51 head of cattle on the place, 32 chickens, 1 gobbler, 2 ducks, 1 turkey hen and four little turkeys, and some pigs.

*　　*　　*

On the ranch 5 weeks yesterday. Dick feeds cattle first time today, as it began snowing yesterday and everything is covered today. To date have shipped 25 gallons cream and made 35 pounds of butter. Baked and churned yesterday.

1916

Blizzard—broke trail to number 4 haystack—worked all day in snow.

*　　*　　*

20 degrees below at night, zero all day. Dick got ice from bridge. Washed curtains. Larson's childrens' horse got loose and stopped here. Ground hog did not see his shadow—snowed all day—14 inches. Churned.

1918

There are depths in each person's being that have never been plumbed. One is surprised to find how much iron he has in his soul in times of stress and strain.

1919

In the winter you just follow the trails.

*　　*　　*

Try to live your ideals, but don't try to apply them to the people around you or force them on others.

*　　*　　*

Remember how many resources you have and remember the story of "Chicken Little".

1920

One must be totally unselfconscious of the impression he makes on others, to be happy or at peace with the world.

* * *

How much of your time you owe to others and of yourself, incidentally, only you can decide. People can despoil, demand your time, scatter your forces, and leave you spent and futile.

1921

When it comes to our troubles, our own ego acts as a magnifying glass.

1924

And, after all, we can't even trust our own judgment too far, for even our judgment, our faith, or our unfaith is tinged by our own moods.

* * *

It is easy to believe that even God made a few mistakes when we look about the world and see the people who are struggling against their own natures.

* * *

It counts very little to youth when things go right. Youth expects the best. Success in youth often becomes arrogance in middle age, and intolerance in old age. It is to the disillusioned, to the tired, the old, that good fortune assumes its true proportions.

I have a belief but very little faith.

* * *

Criticism of others implies a spirit of self-righteousness and is often caused by jealousy.

* * *

Whenever people talk of making a tourist resort of the ranch, I want to go out and post a few more signs.

1925

The mornings when I get up feeling that I want to play a Victrola record before breakfast or when the dawn seems some new marvelous miracle, I'm afraid that now I'm getting older. Moods like that can't last and the reaction takes the spirit out of me.

* * *

The Bible and Nature are not consistent. Great things are never consistent. The moment one ties himself to a creed he is forced to become inconsistent.

* * *

If you've ever been hungry and not had the price of a meal, you'll understand. If you've owed and not had the price to pay, you'll have a glimmering.

* * *

Kindness kindles knowledge. Necessity needs neighbors. Order orients opportunity. Opportunity and order overcome obstacles.

1926

Any friendship that isn't entirely voluntary and spontaneous simply ceases to be after a course of time. That is the secret of perfect friendship, I think, and the moment that any demand enters into it, its perfection diminishes.

* * *

The so-called irreverence of youth of today, I believe, is only a little straighter thinking and plainer talking than the Victorians enjoyed.

* * *

The Senate voted 76-17 for membership in the World Court, with reservations.

* * *

I doubt if any thoughtful person can be happy in the generally accepted sense of the word.

* * *

It isn't work that hurts or tires people. It is the spirit in which one does it. Your muscles and your heart must swing together to do good work.

* * *

I spent the first 40 years of my life overcoming an inferiority complex.

1927

Those who give the hurts suffer so much more than those who receive them. You have to suffer and suffer and suffer before you become a real person.

* * *

To a gambler, it isn't the stake that counts, but the thrill he gets out of it. And so with ranching. The thrill may be at low ebb at 5 o'clock in the morning in winter, when you rattle out with milk pails, but it is there and dormant or you wouldn't be doing it. You'd be living in a steam heated apartment waiting to punch a clock.

*　　*　　*

One can admire the delicacy and intricacy of our language, just as one can enjoy such qualities of nature.

*　　*　　*

Not to shut up the chickens one night or not to put up the cows would seem a luxury.

*　　*　　*

So tired that getting into bed is not an automatic performance. It is the most supremely desirable thing of the whole day. Insomnia? No! I'm not troubled now with it.

*　　*　　*

I wonder in all this welter of work if I can possibly be the woman who was once a girl, who used to have violets and valley lilies given to her. It seems incredible now that anyone should ever have given me violets and valley lilies. Violets and valley lilies! They seem so far away! People who are really living, of course, don't need them nor want them.

1928

Hauled and loaded manure—cleaned barn. Very tired tonight. It pays not to let your vision become obscured by drudgery—to let no part of the work become more important that the whole.

1929

The inertia of middle age is the ever present foe that one must fight as youth goes.

*　　*　　*

The worst part of being a widow is that everyone wishes to arrange your life for you.

*　　*　　*

I believe the people who succeed best use other people's brains as well as their own.

1931

I had rather be a positive devil than a negative angel.

* * *

As Browning put it: "You grew content with your poor degree," content to fall back into the routine or rut of life, as the case may be, free for a while from those disturbing aspirations, and really thankful that the attack of acute high-mindedness did not last longer.

* * *

You have to be hurt enough sometimes to make you remember.

1932

Every so often I revert to type and become a woman.

* * *

Indispensible things weigh us down. All we really need we can load on 2 pack horses. Instead, we make pack horses of ourselves.

* * *

Give me an ideal that will stand the strain of weaving into human stuff on the loom of reality. Keep me from caring more for books than for folks; more for art than for life.

* * *

Cleanliness is undoubtedly next to Godliness, but there are times when I am too ungodly tired to care about either cleanliness or Godliness.

* * *

And so a few moments sober reflection completely killed the spirit of condemnation with me toward others.

1934

If you love things enough, they always bring you to your knees.

* * *

Nothing makes me believe in a Supreme Intelligence as surely as the arrangement of day and night. No matter how discouraged we may have been yesterday, this is a new day—like a fresh sheet of paper to write upon, fraught with possibilities and even surprises. Good resolutions come early in the morning.

* * *

The ocean for meditation—the mountain for inspiration.

* * *

Ask a man's opinion if you want his good-will.

* * *

A person can spread himself too thin and lose the whole flavor and savour of life.

1935

All a person can do is to take a day at a time as it comes. My own life is so full that I am glad to take it a day at a time. A double dose of two days at a time would kill me, I am sure.

* * *

Time clarifies vision, and often leaves us aghast at our own mistakes and misjudgments of others.

1936

If I could write some of the things I think when I am busy about my work! But maybe I keep some of those thoughts that never get on paper. With the paper in front of me, my mind seems to become as blank as the pages before me.

* * *

Parties! I can't get my face fixed right. That's why people have to drink cocktails, etc. And when I get home, I have been so bloomin' pleasant for several hours that I have a bad reaction. So do others! When younger I used to furnish my own spontaneous enthusiasm, but now it takes a good stiff drink.

* * *

Prejudice, that handcuff of the mind.

1937

Money gives you the chance to live graciously, to do little kind things for others, to write letters, notes of thanks, etc. It warps one's personality to be so poor, so driven and so tired.

* * *

It is much easier to act than to think.

*　　*　　*

"You're the kind of a person," he began, and I thought he needn't tell me the sort of person I am because I know that already. I know better than anybody the sort of person I am; I'm better than people think, and worse. Everyone is.

*　　*　　*

The long, long trail that led from cape jasmines and moonlight to this sage brush and barb wire.

1938

Will power has to be driven or it becomes an unmanageable force and rides us to ruin. Out of control, we are at its mercy. I marvel at the people in factories doing mechanical things over and over. At mothers answering the innumberable cries of babies. Personally, I have to perform the impossible feat of keeping my foot on my own neck to force myself to do what is required of me. When I think of the years some friend has spent at work that was not congenial, I am humble with admiration. I couldn't do it. Duty was always a horrible task-master to me. Business that brings me in contact with people I don't like is a nightmare.

1939

God always gives us sense enough and strength enough for what He wants us to do. If we puzzle ourselves or tire ourselves, it is our own fault. Most of us have one talent. If we develop and use it, the returns glorify existence.

*　　*　　*

Never risk the necessary for the superfluous.

*　　*　　*

Would you stand looking into a window of old shop-worn things? Then why dwell on old worn out memories? Even memories of happiness are like faded mementoes. So go to work!

*　　*　　*

If we had to pay for all our mistakes!—all our wrong thinking—all our blunders—what a debt!

*　　*　　*

A porcupine has few friends.

*　　*　　*

A swollen ego is painful—more so than any other swelling.

*　　*　　*

A sense of frustration is apt to lead to desperate remedies, even in mature people.

1940

If you carry the terrible burden, mill stone, of prejudice with you, the weight of it will hold you down.

*　　*　　*

If you know the things a man dreads doing, but that he nevertheless does, then you have the key to his character.

1941

Love: Everyone needs it as flowers need sunshine and rain. I've lived without it for years. There is no synthetic love, and the genuine is very rare.

*　　*　　*

An orderly mind superinduces an orderly life. I determined to chase a few salient facts and deal with them until I found them faulty. Experience multiplied by knowledge of facts equals good judgment.

*　　*　　*

There is one thing you always have complete control of, as long as you are sane and sober—your own thoughts. Nothing else so affects your own future.

1942

The baby is a complex human living laboratory, the soul an uncharted unknown. But the mind is a workshop where a man's own destiny may be served—where the blundering warped past may be repaired and where the present may become sweet and orderly.

*　　*　　*

An over-critical attitude of life is like an active acid in the system. A firm affirmation of the virtues of others surely brings us to a point where belief in God, in yourself, in those around you, and in the future, all of these help to develop peace of mind. Frustration comes readily to those who have not believed enough, who have not reached spiritual maturity.

1943

A proud heritage: When I think of those two from whom I came.

* * *

A whisper can start an avalanche.

* * *

For to be really great, we must be humble, i.e., Thoreau, Emerson, Justice Holmes.

* * *

Words, what beautiful things they are! How they instantly stamp us and give us our exact rating. Only a chance phrase shows a man's bravery or bigotry. The spoken word with its implications, the written word, beautiful with meaning, all the product of that most delicate of all processes: the birth of thought in the brain. A chance phrase may change a person's whole life.

* * *

Those who have been wounded and healed are the strongest, often.

* * *

Don't try to carry but one day's burdens at a time. Yesterday's burdens and tomorrow's burdens and problems make a heavy load. Everyone is carrying a burden, everyone has something to fight.

1944

Life is like a chain set with a few bright jewels.

* * *

Those who do not forgive are simply those who do not understand.

* * *

Time must be budgeted the same as money.

1945

Each person has to protect his own sanctuary, for when it is invaded by too many people, it ceases to be a sanctuary.

To succeed, a man must live as though he expects to die to-morrow, and work as though he expects to live always.

1946

The bitterest of all human experience is the realization that we have failed some one who loves us and needs us.

* * *

Ignorance and prejudice go hand in hand and stubbornness is akin to both.

* * *

Pick out the hardest thing you have to do and do it carefully. It will strengthen your will power.

* * *

Some of the things we are most sure of, we have never seen at all.

1947

Thought is like a flight of butterflies—it passes through the mind but not in the same form and color. If we catch the image the first time, it is apt to be more original.

* * *

No tired person is normal. Thomas A. Kempis said, "Without labor there is no rest", but I think there should be a nice balance between work and rest.

* * *

Even when roused and angry, you can make the retort courteous. "He who ruleth his own spirit. . . ." Nothing is so devastating to self respect as to lose one's poise.

* * *

Creative work comes slowly, after growth and effort.

1948

Emerson says: "No man can come near me but by my own act." He speaks of his mouse-trap. Well, I have a house-trap! And Emerson didn't live in Routt County on a fishing stream, or a river with wild ducks! Any man, when he comes that close to nature begins to strut his stuff and tends to become a primitive he-man.

* * *

After reaching life's mid-mark—a summit before the descent —one tends to take a more adjusted view of the passing scene. By this time, whether one intends it or not, he develops something of a philosophy.

* * *

The best things of life are only momentary. The high moments of life do not last.

* * *

You have to be your own worst task-master, as Emerson says. Your work is like a structure that must be built on solid ground, but paradoxically, into its structure must go a good deal of the stuff that dreams are made of.

* * *

To succeed in your work, it must possess you.

* * *

If you cannot live graciously, at least you can be gracious.

1949

Devotion of animals: "Why couldn't we have loved that way?" —"Because we are only human," said one of the married couple about to separate. They were looking at a dog that would grieve himself to death in their absence.

* * *

In the boasted "good old days," life was less complex, simply because people owned less. So many things people strive for merely weigh them down. If I had my life to live over, I would pattern it to a rule for simplicity. I've learned now to do that, but unfortunately I had already accumulated several tons of impedimenta. Gadgets and gimmicks leave me cold.

1950

Only the low born cry out. A thoroughbred may lose a race, but is never beaten.

* * *

There is enough to fight in our inheritance, natural inhibitions, without carrying a load of unnecessary prejudice and other deterents.

* * *

118

Keep the things of the dead living.

1951

There's time enough for everything. If you get up early enough in the morning, and that priceless time before daylight!—The morning star!

* * *

We give up our dreams for financial security and find that no money can pay us for what we have lost.

* * *

The mild inertia of middle age seemed like mild growing pains compared to the heavy inertia of old age.

1952

The thought that if you are true, you can "celebrate" truly.

* * *

Good humor, the most homespun of all virtues, is one of the rarest.

* * *

Ask a man's opinion and he expands, he suddenly believes in himself, his ego comes to life. We are giving him the chance to reaffirm, reassert himself; and we may learn, too.

1953

The most important thing in your formula for success is to meet and get well acquainted with the most outstanding and important person in your life—yourself!

* * *

If we fasten our thoughts firmly enough on our friends, we forget our resentment and bitterness toward others.

1954

You'd better "let your soul catch up with your body" once in a while. Otherwise both become so tired, bewildered and confused, they might part company permanently.

1955

Try not to overdo. Weariness is almost as bad as illness. It is, indeed, a forerunner of illness, or at least a mild form.

* * *

I am grateful for being waked up to the beauty of life—I mean the beauty of being alive and of keeping or helping to keep other things alive—life in concrete form, which means the creation of beauty.

* * *

If you must worry, then do constructive worrying!

1957

Senator Lyndon Johnson says: "I'm always down to my last dollar and an hour late!" It reassures me to know someone so important could feel that way. He said this just before lambing, at which time every sheep owner is possessed with a feeling of panic and inadequacy. . . . I feel like Mrs. Wigg's mule—so tired I'll have to be pushed over.

* * *

"You can stay on the ranch if you restrict your activities—slow down!" As the days went by, I began to plan.

1959

A woman needs to be loved and loves to be needed.

* * *

When you have reached 78, all you're good for is to be 78, with as much grace as possible. I find that it takes a good deal of grace of God to be 78 graciously.

1962

The mountains for inspirtation, the sea for reflection—"And Christ went alone to a mountain to pray".

"I will look to the mountains from whence cometh my strength"—the dear familiar contour of the hills.

* * *

A dog expects so little, and gives so much. "Few people are worthy of the love and faithfulness of a good dog", I read somewhere.

1963

Mispah: The Lord watch between me and thee while we are absent, one from another.

* * *

Sign off on hurry and worry. Both are futile and are almost synomymous.

1964

"Try me in Thy primal fires and fling me on my way,
Oh! on the anvil of Thy wrath, remake, God, this day."

* * *

". . . Sheep without a shepherd, when the snow shuts out
the sky,

Oh! Why did you leave us? . . . Why did you die?"

1965

You can get a complete evaluation of your own character alone at midnight, in the dark. So, those long hours are not entirely lost to you. Our enforced soul searching is psychic, resulting in a real sense of values.

* * *

Pope John expressed gratitude for the poverty of his boyhood, and said that he was thankful for "the grace of poverty." Personally, I think that one is handicapped in developing a keen sense of appreciation if he has never known the grace of poverty.

* * *

Power and peace combined as sure poise, that most to be desired social asset, in a driven, rushing world. The combination furnishes a perfect equation. It is like an acrostic: backward or forward, the meaning is the same. Peace and power give poise; peace and poise give power; poise and power give peace.

* * *